JENNIFER MARSHALL BLEAKLEY

How a

blind rescue horse

helped others

learn to see

JOEY

The nonfiction imprint of
Tyndale House Publishers, Inc.

Library of Congress Cataloging-in-Publication Data
Names: Bleakley, Jennifer Marshall, author. | Joey (Horse)
Title: Joey : how a blind rescue horse helped others learn to see / Jennifer Marshall Bleakley.
Description: Carol Stream, Illinois : Tyndale House Publishers, Inc., 2018.
Identifiers: LCCN 2017053981| ISBN 9781496421746 (hc) | ISBN 9781496421753 (sc)
Subjects: LCSH: Animals—Religious aspects—Christianity.
Classification: LCC BT746 .B65 2018 | DDC 267/.13—dc23 LC record available at
    https://lccn.loc.gov/2017053981

Printed in the United States of America

24   23   22   21   20   19   18
 7   6   5   4   3   2   1

I dedicate this book to my parents,

Bill and Julie Marshall,

who believed that I could do this long before I ever did.

———·•·———

And to anyone who feels trapped in

darkness, hopelessness, or pain,

I pray that through this story you will see

a glimmer of light and the fingerprints of hope.

JOEY'S TIME AT HOPE REINS is presented as accurately as possible, based on interviews and memories of those involved with his rescue, care, and training. Some names and identifying details of people have been changed out of respect for their privacy or are composites of several different individuals' experiences. A few events and timelines have been combined and compressed for brevity, with certain liberties taken to tell a more cohesive story. As I write this, a number of the horses that were part of Joey's story still reside at Hope Reins.

Jennifer Marshall Bleakley

Just ask the animals, and they will teach you.
    Ask the birds of the sky, and they will tell you.
Speak to the earth, and it will instruct you.
JOB 12:7-8

PROLOGUE

THE RAIN CAME DOWN in sheets as Penny turned onto the long gravel drive she shared with a neighboring horse farm. After two months away from her Virginia home while she cared for her dying mother in Florida, the sprawling green pasture was a welcome sight. As she made her way up the drive, a group of horses came into view.

That's odd, she thought. *What are they doing outside in such a terrible storm?* Slowing down ever so slightly, she leaned forward, straining to see through the rain. Suddenly, her eyes widened.

"Oh my goodness!" she gasped. Slamming on the brakes, she quickly turned her pickup around and drove straight up the farm's private drive, blatantly ignoring the No Trespassing sign.

Throwing open the metal gate, she trudged through the mud and muck toward the herd of horses. When she got within a few yards of them, she stopped dead in her tracks. The horses were completely emaciated, some barely able to stand. Next to them, beneath an ancient oak, two horses lay motionless, their manes matted with mud, their midsections grotesquely inverted. Her stomach churned.

What happened here?

Taking shelter under the tree, she pulled out her phone and dialed 9-1-1.

"9-1-1, what's your emergency?"

"Yes, I'm calling from the Nash farm off US 60 in Powhatan County," Penny began, her voice shaking. "There are several badly emaciated horses out in the field, and some of them appear to be dead."

"How many dead horses are there?" the operator asked matter-of-factly.

"At least two," she replied, glancing around the pasture, her eyes settling on the stables off in the distance.

"Okay, ma'am, someone from the sheriff's department and animal control will be there shortly."

After thanking the dispatcher, Penny tucked her phone into her coat pocket and headed toward the stables. "Please, God, don't let there be any more like these in there," she prayed.

Cold rain pelted her face as she forced her legs to carry her toward the open-air stalls at the top of a gentle hill. Off to the side stood a ranch-style house. One of the shutters hung askew, and the lower portion of a window had been boarded up.

She couldn't remember the last time she had seen the owner—a man who made a hobby of collecting horses he thought he could sell at a higher price.

Did he just get tired of it and take off? Her mind wandered back to the dead and dying animals in the pasture. *How could anyone do that?*

Wrapping her raincoat tightly around her, she quickened her pace. A fire burned in her stomach. Never had she felt so angry. As she neared the stables, she saw that empty feedboxes dotted the area and the November grass was almost bare. *When was the last time these poor animals were fed?*

When she finally reached the four wooden stalls, she took a deep breath and willed herself to look inside. All of them were empty. *Thank God*, she breathed. Then, just as she was about to turn and leave, she saw a hoof sticking out from behind the end stall.

"No, no, no, no, no . . ." she begged as she ran to the fallen horse.

She dropped to her knees, mud and manure seeping into her jeans. Her heart caught in her throat. She recognized the familiar short blond tail of the horse she had loved to visit through the adjoining fence. His sweet personality reminded her of a horse she had ridden as a child. Tears welling in her eyes, she gingerly touched the horse's side. Each rib protruded beneath the skin. She quickly jerked her hand away. The rain fell harder now, and muddy streaks flowed down the animal's body, revealing glimpses of the white-and-black polka-dotted coat hidden beneath the crusted-on mud and filth.

Three dead, she lamented.

The silence was broken by the sound of the front gate slamming shut. The authorities had arrived. Penny stood and headed back down to the pasture to meet them. She was soaked from head to foot and smelled of manure, but she didn't care.

Animal control workers had already begun guiding weak horses onto trailers, while others unloaded equipment to transport the dead. As she stood shivering in the rain while answering the sheriff's questions, a shout pierced the melancholy air. "Hey! This one is still alive!"

Penny dashed back to the stalls, where an animal control officer held his hand against the fallen horse's spotted nose.

"Are you sure?" she asked eagerly.

The young officer looked up at her, smiling. Rain dripped from his blue cap.

"Yes. I can feel air coming from his nostrils, and I can hear a faint heartbeat."

"Oh, thank God!" she said, fighting back tears.

"Ma'am, do you know the owner of this farm?" the sheriff asked.

Penny heard his question, but she couldn't take her eyes off the horse. He was alive! The sweet creature was still alive.

"Ma'am?" The sheriff looked at Penny's face and tried again. "Do you know this horse?"

For the second time in less than an hour, Penny dropped to her knees beside the animal.

"I do," she said, gently touching the horse's face, realizing she would likely never see him again. "His name is Joey."

CHAPTER I

KIM TSCHIRRET HAD no idea if she was doing the right thing. She anxiously balled her hands into fists in her jacket pockets and chewed her bottom lip as she waited in the barn.

"I'm so nervous," she whispered to her friend Barb Foulkrod, who had generously agreed to make the early morning drive from North Carolina to Virginia to pick up the horse Kim couldn't stop talking about. When they arrived, Tom Comer, the owner of the sprawling Virginia farm, greeted them warmly. Tom had his own horses but also fostered animals in need for the Equine Rescue League.

Barb laid a calming hand on Kim's back. She and Kim, both in their early forties and both wearing their blonde hair in low ponytails, could have easily passed for sisters.

"Trust your gut, Kim," she whispered back.

Trust. Barb made it sound so easy.

In theory, giving a permanent home to a recently rescued horse was a no-brainer. After all, the horse therapy ranch Kim owned in Raleigh needed more horses. But *this* horse? Maybe she *had* been too rash.

When the stable door opened, out stepped the most beautiful, albeit terribly thin, horse Kim had ever seen. Her breath caught as she inhaled. He was magnificent. Head held high. Creamy blond mane blowing in the gentle breeze. He looked positively regal.

"Oh my . . ." she breathed out.

She had seen Appaloosas before. In fact, there was another one waiting impatiently in the borrowed horse trailer parked in the driveway. She had always loved the breed, with their richly spotted coats, freckled noses, and humanlike eyes, but she had never seen one like this before. A leopard Appaloosa, his white coat was dotted with hundreds of black ink spots. Smaller ones packed close together in the front, while larger ones spread out around the back. His markings reminded Kim of a Dalmatian's coat.

"Well, here he is," Tom announced. "Meet Joey."

Kim and Barb slowly approached, and Kim gently held her hand under the horse's nose in a nonthreatening greeting. "Hi, Joey. It's nice to meet you."

The Appaloosa breathed in her scent, then exhaled his greeting. His pink-and-black-freckled lips rooted around her closed fist, looking for hidden tidbits. Kim reached up to stroke his large cheek, her index finger stopping on several different-sized spots—a large one with a deep black center surrounded by a lighter ring, a medium-sized pear-shaped one, and finally several small ones that all blended together, turning a patch of his white coat gray.

"You are so beautiful," she said, moving closer.

Joey lowered his head, his cheek briefly touching hers. Kim drew in a quick breath. The movement, the moment, felt almost reverent. Woman and horse stood together for several heartbeats before Joey lowered his head further in search of a clump of grass.

"Tom, thank you so much for thinking of us," Kim said. "I still don't know if we're ready for this, but there's just something about this one—I can almost feel it."

Tom nodded. "Trust me, I get it. This boy is special, no doubt about it. But I have to confess, you were actually the seventh place I called that day. I reached out to every contact I have, but nobody wanted him. 'Too much work,' everyone said."

Kim felt a pang of fear. *Was* it going to be too much work? She had spoken several times to Tom since that first call, asking countless questions about Joey's care. But did she really have any idea what she was getting into? Probably not. Yet all she had to do was look at him. She couldn't imagine not taking him now.

"I honestly thought about just keeping him here," Tom continued. "I mean, we have the room and all." He motioned to the large stable and pastures behind him. "But after I saw him with my kids, saw what he was capable of, I knew that he belonged somewhere he could make a real difference. When my friend Eddie told me about your ranch, I knew that's where Joey needed to be."

Kim had been praying for weeks over this horse, asking God if she was doing the right thing for Hope Reins, the equine therapy ranch she had started just over a year ago. Now, in February 2011, they already had eight horses and three dozen volunteers, but when Tom called her out of the blue to tell her about Joey, she agreed to take him, sight unseen—something she'd *never* done before.

Each of the other horses at Hope Reins had been carefully chosen. Potential horses were observed and discussed by the staff for days—sometimes weeks or months—before they were selected as candidates for the herd, a unique group comprised of several horses who had been rescued from dire situations. Both from countless hours of research and from personal experience, Kim had found that when troubled or hurting children worked with horses who had also known pain or abuse, a deep and profound bond was often formed.

However, since the ranch was dedicated to pairing horses with hurting children, Kim had to be sure that a horse would work well with children before taking it on, and not every horse met that standard.

Over the past few months, Kim had passed on several horses because they did not have the temperament needed to work one-on-one with a child. If a horse was too aggressive, too fearful, or in need of more rehab than Kim and her helpers could handle, it didn't make the cut. It always broke her heart to say no to a horse, but she had to consider the welfare of the children. She couldn't afford to take a horse on a whim.

When Tom called and mentioned that his five-year-old was riding Joey bareback, Kim agreed to take him on the spot. Still, the Appaloosa had unique needs of his own that concerned the Hope Reins board of directors. *Who could blame them?* Kim thought. It wasn't every day you found yourself caring for a blind horse.

Blind.

The word *had* given Kim pause. Still, Joey needed a home, and for some reason she couldn't explain, she felt strongly that

Hope Reins needed Joey. So, even though she had no idea how they would raise the three thousand dollars they would need every year for his basic care, she had readily agreed to take him.

Joey's head was lowered over a clump of grass, his lips nibbling individual blades. Barb and Kim listened to Tom recount how he became involved with Joey. "So you've had Joey for two months?" Barb asked.

"That's right. When he was first rescued, Joey needed a lot of rehab," Tom said, absently stroking Joey's back. "He initially stayed with a vet who runs a foster ranch. She was able to get a little bit of weight back on him. She's also the one who realized he's blind."

"Was the blindness due to malnourishment?"

Tom shrugged his shoulders. "Not really sure. Vet said that this breed is pretty susceptible to eye problems—cataracts and moon blindness and such. She sees evidence of both in Joey."

Kim searched Joey's almond-shaped eyes. He didn't look different from any other horse she had seen. His eyes weren't cloudy, nor were they fixed on some point beyond her. Instead, his eyes—his gaze—seemed to meet her own. But Kim also knew looks could be deceiving. Some scars go unseen.

"Last time we spoke, you mentioned that Joey had been a champion jumper. Can you tell me any more about that?" Kim asked, eager to learn as much as possible about her soon-to-be resident.

Joey took several steps forward to another patch of grass while Tom told Kim and Barb everything he knew about Joey's backstory. A friend had seen Joey compete years ago as a skilled jumper and well-decorated competitor in show hunting and dressage, and he knew Joey and his rider were on their way to qualifying for the Olympics. But then the horse suffered an injury that ended his competitive career. Eventually, Joey was sold to a mother and daughter who boarded him at the friend's stable.

Tom reached into his pocket and pulled out a carrot chunk. He clucked his tongue. Joey lifted his large head and gingerly took the offered treat.

"Anyway, I guess after a couple years, the woman got divorced and they had to sell Joey. Sometime after that he ended up with the horse hoarder. That's pretty much all I know."

Kim could have listened to Tom talk about Joey all day, but they still had a three-hour drive ahead of them and she wanted to unload the new horses before dark.

Kim wished she had more time to ask Tom about Joey's day-to-day care. He had given her several helpful tips on the phone; suggestions like pairing Joey with a companion horse as soon as possible, moving hay boxes and water troughs next to the fence so he wouldn't walk into them, and walking him along the perimeter of his pasture. But was it enough?

Kim took a deep breath. "You have no idea how grateful we are for all you have done. Please come visit us at Hope Reins sometime."

"I'd like that," Tom said, handing Joey's lead rope to Kim and giving Joey a final scratch between his ears. "He's all yours."

A moment of fear gripped Kim. A chant of what-ifs in her mind almost loosened her hand on the rope. As if sensing Kim's panic, Barb put her arm around her friend. *Yes*, Kim thought, *I can do this.*

As they approached the horse trailer, the sound of stomping hooves and a loud, agitated whinny from inside made them abruptly stop. Joey's ears flew forward as if to say, *What's that?*

"That's Speckles," Kim offered. "He's an Appaloosa, too, but a rather unhappy one at the moment, it seems. I'm sure he'll settle down once we get on our way." *At least I hope so.* The truth was that Speckles had been nothing but difficult since she and Barb picked him up. She hoped she wasn't wrong about that one.

Once Joey was secured in the trailer, while he and Speckles assessed one another, Tom patted Joey's rump.

"Go do lots of good, Joey."

Yes, Kim thought as the farm disappeared behind them, *Joey has quite a story.*

Thankfully, it hadn't ended too soon.

CHAPTER 2

THREE HOURS LATER, the Tahoe pulling the horse trailer turned onto the gravel road leading into Hope Reins—twenty acres of sprawling oak trees, wide-open pastures, white horse fencing, and meandering woods, nestled off Highway 50 in North Raleigh. Tall pines, standing as sentinels, cast long shadows along the winding drive.

"Welcome home, boys," Kim said, stealing a glance at their two travel companions in the rearview mirror. "You're going to love it here."

Just to the right of the drive was Hope Reins' largest pasture, where the bigger geldings, Deetz and Cody, were kept. The six-acre pasture contained a run-in shelter, several deep-water troughs, and a wooded area that offered welcome shade. Kim's favorite feature? A twelve-foot-tall white wooden cross, a visual reminder that Hope Reins was—quite literally—a gift from God.

The idea for Hope Reins had been inspired by the book *Hope Rising*, Kim Meeder's story of the organization she started in Oregon that paired emotionally wounded children with rescued horses. Kim read the book twice in one week, fascinated by the concept. Page after page painted pictures of children forming relationships with horses—horses who acted like mirrors for them. Not only would wounded children see parts of their own stories in a wounded horse, but because horses tend to reflect what they are seeing, children learned things about themselves as they cared for their horses.

It was a dynamic Kim understood all too well. While growing up with an emotionally distant, alcoholic father and a mother who enabled his behavior, Kim found the unconditional love she longed for in her beloved Saddlebred horse, Country. Kim's father continually pushed her into competitions, always wanting her to perform, to stand out—to make himself look good. But all Kim wanted was to hide away with her horse, spending hours riding, brushing, and talking with her equine friend. In an environment that often felt unsafe and uncertain, Country gave Kim the stability and acceptance she craved. Or at least he did until her father sold him when she went away to college.

Many years later, Kim had almost forgotten how much Country had meant to her in those formative years. But recently, when Kim was reeling from the death of her mother, a friend convinced her to begin riding again. She found it healing and therapeutic. The more she rode, the more she wondered if God had a greater purpose in mind for her.

One day at the library, Kim found herself typing the words *Jesus and horses* into the online catalog. There she found the book by another woman named Kim. *God does work in mysterious ways.* She soon found that she couldn't stop thinking about starting a similar program in Raleigh.

Granted, the idea seemed far-fetched. She had only just recently gotten back into riding, and she didn't have the slightest idea how to run a fully functioning ranch. Not that it mattered. Before you could *run* a ranch, you had to *have* a ranch.

"I'm just a stay-at-home mom," Kim had lamented to her friend Lori one sunny afternoon at Chick-fil-A, as they sat watching their children romp around the large indoor play area. "God wouldn't really be calling *me* to do something like this, would he? I mean, I haven't worked since Chance was born," she said, smiling at her five-year-old son. He turned at the sound of his name before running to catch up to his almost four-year-old sister, Isabel. "I'm probably just reacting to the book, right?"

Lori had patiently listened as Kim shared about her past, the book, and the crazy dream of creating a place for children and horses to help each other. Finding herself out of words, Kim took a deep breath and waited. She valued Lori's opinion, as both a friend and a spiritual mentor.

"I think it's a great idea, Kim," Lori said.

Kim's eyes widened.

"I mean, you obviously are passionate about this. You have personal experience with horses, and you have a husband who adores and supports you." Lori sat back and studied her friend. "Go for it. If it is God's will, then he will make it happen."

Is it really that simple? Just trust God and start working toward making the idea a reality? Kim left Chick-fil-A that day both excited and terrified. There was just one last thing to do—make sure her husband, Mike, was on board.

"Are you really serious about this?" Mike asked later that night after the kids were tucked in. "I know you've been thinking about it for a while—in fact, you haven't talked about much else—but are you really sure you know what you're taking on?"

"I think I am," Kim replied, looking down at her tightly folded hands. "I mean, it's been a month, and I still can't let go of this idea. I've prayed about it, *we've* prayed about it, I've talked to my sister, to Lori, and to Pastor Scott. And then today my devotional reading included 2 Corinthians 1:3-4: 'God is our merciful Father and the source of all comfort. He comforts us in all our troubles so that we can comfort others.'" Kim turned to face her husband as they sat together on the sofa.

"What if God allowed me to be comforted by Country so that one day I would be able to help other kids be comforted by horses too?"

She drew her legs up underneath her. It was so easy to talk to Mike. It always had been, from the first time they met more than fifteen years ago.

"I even thought of a name for the ranch!" she said, then paused for dramatic effect.

"Well, don't leave me hanging."

"Hope Reins. You know, spelled like 'horse reins,' but sounding like 'God reigns.' What do you think?"

Mike was quiet for a moment. Kim held her breath. His opinion was so important to her. *What if he doesn't like the name?*

"I think it's absolutely perfect, babe. I say . . . let's do it," Mike said, his gaze tender.

"Wait! For real? Are *you* serious?" Kim laughed.

"I've never seen you like this before. You're different. Energized. There's something going on here. So yeah, let's see where it goes."

"But it's going to be a big change for our family," Kim pointed out. "I know your new marketing position lets you work from home, but it's not like you can watch the kids and do your work. And we can't afford a nanny for Isabel and Chance until they start school! And the up-front costs . . . we don't have that much in our savings account, and . . . Mike, is this crazy? How are we going to do this?"

Mike took his wife's hands. "Slow down and take a breath. We obviously have a lot to figure out, but let's just try to take it one step at a time for now, okay? You want this. You can do this. So we will figure it out."

He looked her in the eyes. "I believe in you."

———•———

Of course, dreaming about something is one thing. Actually making it happen is something altogether different.

First things first. After doing the math—at least one and a half acres per horse—Kim figured she would need twenty acres for a decent-sized ranch. But finding twenty acres of affordable, usable land in the North Raleigh area was easier dreamed than realized.

Over and over, Kim was told, "You'll never find the land for that" or "That much land will cost you a fortune."

"If I had a dollar for every time I've been told, 'You'll never find the land,' I could purchase half of North Carolina!" Kim confided to Mike after checking out another disappointing lead.

Several weeks later, Kim started second-guessing the idea: *Is this really what you want me to do, God?* Discouraged and weary, she decided to put things on hold for a few days and take Chance and Isabel to an Easter egg hunt hosted by a local church at their off-site property, only fifteen minutes from her house.

As she and her kids walked to the large crowd gathered near a sprawling oak tree, Kim couldn't help but take in the entire scene. The colored eggs were scattered in a mowed field, while a handful of horses grazed in adjacent pastures. There appeared to be two access roads, and another overgrown field on the property. *What is this place?*

"Mama! They're starting," Chance shouted, tugging on her hand. "Hurry! The eggs are gonna be all gone."

"Yes! Let's go," she said, grabbing her kids' small hands and dashing into the frenzy.

After ten minutes of zigzagging around the field to grab plastic eggs, Chance's and Isabel's baskets were full.

"Can Isabel and I go play for a while, Mama?" Chance asked, spotting several bounce houses near the parking lot.

"Of course. I'll stand right here and hold your baskets." As she watched Chance and Isabel, a man with a pleasant smile approached her and introduced himself. "Hello, I'm Will Warren, business administrator at Bay Leaf Baptist Church. I'm so glad you were able to come to our event. I hope your children enjoyed the egg hunt." After exchanging a few more pleasantries, he turned to greet other visitors but stopped when Kim blurted out, "Does your church own all of this land?"

The man studied Kim's face for a moment before answering. "We sure do. It was gifted to us about a year ago by one of our longtime members. She didn't have any relatives and decided to leave her family's land to us in her will. It's a beautiful property," he continued, scanning the area. "But I have to confess, seventy acres is a bit much for us. We really aren't sure what to do with it, other than host a massive Easter egg hunt every year," he added with a wink.

Kim's heart was beating so loudly that she thought the church staff member couldn't help but hear it. "Yes. It truly is beautiful," she replied.

As she led her children back to the parking lot, Kim looked more closely at the surroundings. There was no fencing, no plumbing, and too many trees, but somehow she knew. *This could work.* In her mind's eye, she could picture a riding arena at the far end of the property and a feed shed by the parking lot. She could easily imagine sectioned-off pastures and hitching posts throughout the landscape. But seventy acres in such a prime location? A quick Google search on her phone revealed the discouraging truth: The estimated value for the land was 7 million dollars! *Well, it could have been perfect*, Kim thought as she buckled her daughter into her car seat. Yet as the day went on, she just couldn't shake the feeling that the church property would be a perfect fit. And so, even though she had no reason to think it could work, she decided to reach out to Will Warren at the church. If nothing else, it would be good practice going forward. After getting the kids settled for their rest time, she sat down at her computer and began typing a four-page proposal, outlining her vision for the ministry and a mission statement.

When Mike came in from mowing the lawn, Kim handed him a glass of water and the proposal. "Will you take a look at this?" she asked.

"This is good, Kim," he said, still scanning the pages. "Really good. But since when do you have a mission statement?"

"Since about ten minutes ago," she said, laughing.

"Our vision is to provide true hope and real healing for every child," Mike read out loud. "Our mission will be to provide comfort to hurting children and their families by providing one-on-one sessions between caring leaders and extraordinary 'equine counselors,' many of whom will be rescued horses and those who have faced abuse and neglect themselves. All services will be free of charge."

Kim saw the question in her husband's eyes even before he said anything. "Have you really thought that last sentence through? I know we discussed it, but how are you going to fulfill your mission if you aren't bringing in any money?"

Kim had spent many hours thinking about that same point. But she had done enough research and talked to enough social workers and ministry leaders to know that the kids with the greatest needs would likely be the least able to pay. Yes, offering free services meant more work for her—putting together fund-raisers and applying for grants—but she was willing to do everything possible to make it free.

"To be honest, I don't exactly know how it's all going to work out, but I am choosing to trust God on this one."

Kim noticed Mike's shoulders tensing ever so slightly, and her heart went out to him. *I know this seems risky.*

"All right then, let's see what happens."

Two days later, Kim was sitting next to Will Warren in his church office.

"Thank you so much for meeting with me," she began, trying to keep her trembling hands out of sight. "I wanted to talk to you about an idea and how your property on Creedmoor Road might fit in. Here's the proposal for you to review." As he read, Kim tried to gauge his reaction. Had she been foolish to come here?

The business administrator laid the document down and smiled. "This sounds like quite an undertaking," he said, rising from his seat and walking toward his desk. "And definitely one we could use around here." He rustled through several drawers before returning to the chair next to Kim. He unrolled a large sheet of paper on the coffee table. A property map!

"This shows the property lines, easements, and access roads," Will explained, pointing to different markings. "This area is where we had the egg hunt. Over here is where we keep a house for missionaries on sabbatical. And this section is used once a year for a youth retreat. The rest of the acreage is untouched. It definitely would need to be cleared. And I imagine it would take a lot to get it ready for a herd of horses."

Kim's eyes darted back and forth; she had certainly seen similar maps these past months in her quest to find land. She was so absorbed in mentally tracing the property lines that she almost missed Will's question.

"So would these twenty acres be enough?"

When his question finally connected with her brain, Kim nearly shouted.

"Enough? It would be perfect!"

"Now, the church can't sell you the land—it's a condition of the will—but I will propose to our senior pastor and the elders that we lease the property to you. Is that okay with you?"

"Are you serious?" Kim asked, tears of joy pooling in her eyes.

"I am quite serious," Will assured her. "I'll run it past the elders tonight at our monthly meeting," he said. "And they'll need to agree to the terms."

Kim caught her breath. *The terms.* Twenty acres of prime real estate in a quickly growing community could easily lease for ten times what she could afford. Kim smiled politely at Will, thanked him for his time, and said she would look forward to his call.

Oh, well. At least I got to practice my business proposal on someone.

The next afternoon, as Kim was surfing through real estate websites, her cell phone rang.

"Kim, how does a dollar a month sound?" Will Warren asked.

"I'm sorry. A dollar a month for what?"

"For you to lease our land," Will chuckled. "Twenty acres— a dollar a month. Does that work for you?"

Kim was glad she was sitting down because she suddenly felt light-headed.

"You mean we can use the land for just one dollar a month?"

"Our church believes in what you want to do, Kim, and we would be honored to support you and Hope Reins."

Kim found herself at a loss for words. How do you say thank you for such a lavish gift?

Finally, she stammered, "I . . . how can I possibly? I never imagined . . . oh my goodness. Thank you so much!"

"You are most welcome. Now you go find some of those equine counselors you mentioned and get to work helping those kids, okay? When you stop by Bay Leaf to review and sign the document, I'll introduce you to our senior pastor, Marty Jacumin."

"Yes, sir," Kim said, ending the call with a joyful laugh.

"You never cease to amaze me, God," she prayed, with tears streaming down her cheeks. "You took what everyone said would be the hardest obstacle and crossed it right off the list!"

Suddenly, Kim wasn't alone. Chance and Isabel had wandered into the back bedroom because they heard her voice. A moment later, Mike appeared, ready to shoo the kids away so Kim could finish the call. But when he saw the tears, he immediately wrapped his arms around her.

"I'm so sorry it didn't work out," he said, brushing the hair away from her eyes.

"Didn't work out?" Kim laughed. "The church is letting us use the land for a dollar a month!"

The look on Mike's face was priceless.

"God did it! We have a place for Hope Reins."

———

Over the next several months, the real work began. First there was a mountain of paperwork to fill out and file in order to become an incorporated 501(c) organization. Then there was insurance to buy, something Kim hadn't realized would be so costly.

"We are in the same category of risk as those guys who clean the windows on skyscrapers!" Kim lamented to Mike after meeting with an insurance representative. But the insurance needed to be in place even before the improvements on the property began.

The physical changes were extensive—clearing the land and installing fencing. And while the labor was free, courtesy of church friends and willing neighbors, it seemed that every time she turned around, Kim needed to pull out her new credit card reserved solely for Hope Reins–related purchases. The expenses kept coming, and Kim was getting more and more nervous. She fought hard to keep costs down as much as possible, borrowing some equipment like horse trailers and looking for a good bargain tractor on Craigslist.

Fencing material was another nightmare, because of the sheer amount needed to enclose the pastures. Wood and traditional PVC horse fencing were out of the question because of the cost. After researching other options, Kim decided to use a combination of flexible fencing material that looked like thin strips of PVC and coated wire. It wouldn't be as picturesque as the high-end horse farms in the area, but it would keep the Hope Reins herd safe.

Every day seemed to bring a new expense, a new need, and a new problem—more than Kim could handle herself. She formed a board of directors made up of business-savvy people that met twice a month to help her with the bigger financial decisions.

Before a single horse stepped onto the property, things had to be checked off a never-ending list. Storage sheds for feed, supplements, and equipment; hitching posts; water troughs and hay boxes. Kim was spending more and more time away from home, which made for some interesting childcare situations as she and Mike adjusted to their new normal.

"We can't possibly afford full-time childcare while you're still trying to get things up and running," Mike commented one evening, after Kim suggested they hire a temporary nanny.

"Well, I can't watch them and oversee the work at the ranch," she shot back without even thinking.

"And I can't have them running around the house all day while I'm on the phone in meetings. Working from home means I'm *working* at home," Mike said in exasperation. "We have to figure something out."

Kim sighed. Mike was right, of course. But it was one more

thing to figure out, one more thing to schedule, one more request for help. Some days Kim brought the kids with her; some days her sister, Christy, or various friends helped out; and other days Mike watched them from home while he worked. It wasn't ideal, it wasn't easy, but they somehow made it work.

As word of Hope Reins began to circulate among Kim's friends, the church leasing them the property, and her kids' preschool playgroups, more and more volunteers started showing up for Saturday "barn chore days." Friends, acquaintances, and strangers helped clear land, build sheds, construct fences, paint wooden surfaces, and even donate a little money. It was humbling to have so many people helping bring Hope Reins to life. Kim had never been more exhausted than during the seven months it took to get the property ready to receive their first horse—Gabe.

Gabe was a Shetland pony who had been used for children's birthday parties before his owner sold her farm and donated him to a rescue shelter. Kim had discovered him on the shelter's website, still full of life and spunk. When she met Gabe, it was love at first sight. The walnut-brown pony with the blond mane belonged at Hope Reins.

He was quickly followed by an older gelding named Sonny, who was rescued from going to an auction. Barb had found out about the Palomino quarter horse in need of a home, and he was quickly added to the Hope Reins family. For several months, Gabe and Sonny were the sole residents, which was a good thing considering that the staff consisted of Kim and Barb, neither of whom were being paid.

It wasn't as if Kim hadn't tried to pay her friend.

"You will not pay me a dime!" Barb would continually answer when Kim would broach the subject again. "I believe in this and am delighted to help. Money will come, but for now, being here is all I need."

It took months to figure out a routine; Kim lost count of how many times she and Barb had both fed the horses, without knowing the other one had. Or worse, sometimes neither of them fed the horses at all! There was much to learn and much that was needed. But in September 2010 they believed they were ready to hang a wooden sign by the busy highway. The sign simply said Hope Reins of Raleigh, with the silhouette of a horse and a child. With the exception of a little blurb in the newspaper about their new endeavor, the sign was the sole extent of their marketing strategy. Amazingly, that little sign brought more and more volunteers, as well as their first session referral.

Of course, as sessions—the heartbeat of Hope Reins— became a reality, so did the need for training. All the session leaders were volunteers with horse experience and a desire to help hurting children. Kim would always start a training session with the statement "At Hope Reins, the horses are the counselors, not the humans," making it clear that the adults were simply facilitators between the horse and the child. Yet it was important that the adults be prepared for working with hurting, and often vulnerable, children. Thankfully, Kim's good friend Lori was a social worker with a gift for training and equipping lay leaders, and her expertise was invaluable.

From money to resources to training, there was always so much to consider. It had been a long road, but all the blood, sweat, and tears she'd invested in the ranch had been more than worth it.

Hope Reins had become a beacon of hope—an oasis where hurting children could come and find peace amidst the turmoil of their everyday lives. A place where they could feel safe. A place where, if just for an hour, they could simply be kids, and enjoy a relationship with a horse who would love them—unconditionally. And a place where all the horses would receive unconditional love from those who cared for them.

CHAPTER 3

As Kim slowly maneuvered the SUV to the pasture where a team of volunteers waited to help unload Speckles and Joey, she couldn't help but notice the tractor. *Out of service again.* The rust-covered machine used to haul hay, heavy equipment, and manure always seemed to be breaking down for one reason or another. Parts of the fence needed mending between the parking lot and the front pasture too. Though the church's generous offer made it possible for Kim to pay for the land out of the ministry's spare change, there never seemed to be a shortage of expenses—repairs, hay, grain, supplements, insurance premiums, mulch, monthly farrier fees, and countless vet bills. After all, rescued horses were not the healthiest horses.

God provided the land, Kim continually reminded herself. *He will provide for the rest.* "God will provide" had become something of a mantra for Kim this past year and a half. She determined to say it until she started believing it—especially given the fact that things were starting to get a little tense at home. Mike kept running the numbers and was growing more and more concerned about the ranch's finances. When he would bring it up, Kim's answer was always the same: "God will provide," although recently it was sounding more like a question than a statement.

God had also provided volunteers, horses, children, and several generous donations that had kept them going this long. However, though she didn't publicize it, the ranch was almost bankrupt. And while the board had suggested charging a minimal fee for sessions, Kim just couldn't. She had felt a strong call from God to keep the sessions free, and she was determined to do so. However, she did agree to place a donation bucket out during sessions for those who wanted to contribute something. Yes, they had enough money to last the next three months, but after that . . . well, Kim couldn't think about that right now.

Trust and worry. Worry and trust. It was a never-ending cycle Kim wished she could break.

Pulling up to the gate, she forced herself to slow her breathing and relax her shoulders. *Yes, God* will *provide*, she murmured quietly.

But first things first. It was time to introduce Speckles and Joey to their new home.

Kim and Barb were more than happy to get out of the SUV and stretch after the long drive. Four volunteers, who had all been briefed on both horses' histories, including Joey's unique challenges, anxiously awaited the new residents.

"Did they give you any trouble, Kim?" Carla asked.

"Define *trouble*," Kim said, winking at Barb.

"Uh-oh. What happened?"

"Oh, nothing we won't be able to handle," Kim responded. "One of them is just a little bit temperamental, but I'm sure he'll be fine once he gets settled in." Kim turned her attention to the rest of the group.

"Thank you all for coming out this afternoon to help welcome our new 'angels in horsehair.'" She loved using that description for the Hope Reins horses. "I can't tell you how much we appreciate each and every one of you."

Kim's gaze landed on Lauren Mattea, a feeding team volunteer who was starting to develop an interest in horse training. The woman seemed to have a sweet and fun-loving spirit, though at times she also came across as somewhat guarded. *I'll invite her out for coffee sometime so we can get to know each other.*

Also in attendance were Jo Anne, a fun-loving grandmother and the mother hen of the Hope Reins team; Carla, a thin, athletic woman with grown children; and PJ, a spunky brunette whose teenage sons kept her so busy that the ranch was her quiet haven where she could escape.

Kim unlocked the trailer door for the big reveal—Joey's and Speckles' backsides. A chorus of oohs and ahhs erupted from the group.

Kim laughed at the response. "If you guys think they look good from this angle, wait until you see them from the front!"

With the ramp down, Kim easily backed Joey out of the side-by-side trailer, and Barb walked him several feet away to a patch of grass in front of the small red building that served as the Hope Reins office. Jo Anne and Carla immediately began stroking and patting the newest Hope Reins resident.

Joey happily grazed, periodically raising his head to take in the scents of his admirers and his surroundings.

Speckles was a different story. As soon as Kim approached

him with the lead line, an earsplitting whinny exploded from the trailer.

"You're okay, boy," she said softly. "This is your new home."

Kim's gentle voice did nothing to calm the stomping, nostril-flaring horse. He was agitated and fearful.

"Come on, Speckles," she urged. "You can do this. We just want to get you out of the trailer. It's just a couple of steps back."

The horse tossed his head and snapped his teeth. He didn't bite her or really even come close to her skin, but the unexpected action made her jerk backward. Speckles eyed her warily. It took a moment for her to catch her breath. *He was so calm at the foster farm when I visited*, Kim thought. *Maybe he's just releasing pent-up stress.*

"Need some help?" Lauren asked, poking her head into the trailer.

"Maybe?" Yes, the truth was, Kim *did* want help. But she didn't want to put any of her volunteers in harm's way. "He's really not happy at the moment."

Lauren stepped cautiously into the empty side of the trailer, moving with a slight limp toward Speckles.

"Hey, Speckles," she said, bravely holding her hand under the horse's nose to say hello.

"I wouldn't . . ." Kim started to caution the new volunteer, but before she could finish, the horse reacted. He lowered his dark brown head curiously, his ears flicking forward. Then he snorted onto Lauren's hand, threw his head up and away from both women, and startled them with a loud whinny.

"Well," Lauren offered, "I don't know much about horse training, but is it possible he's just a bit overwhelmed? Maybe a snack would help move him along."

"Can't hurt," Kim said, willing to try anything. "Stay here and I'll grab a carrot."

Kim was glad for the break. It had been an exhausting day, and they still had to get the horses situated—that is, if they could get the cantankerous one out of the trailer.

Needing a moment to collect herself, Kim went the long way, across the parking lot, past Joey, and around the stone fire pit in the center of the common area.

When Kim got to the feed shed, she tugged hard on the door, leaving it open for light to filter in. There was no electricity on the ranch aside from a small generator, used in the summer to power a window air-conditioning unit in their makeshift office, in the winter to power a single light bulb in the feed shed, and year-round to power the low-voltage electric fencing. But they had made do.

In fact, operating on such a shoestring budget meant there were few amenities on the ranch. For one thing, the only bathroom was a leased porta-potty. No one complained, but Kim felt compelled to remind everyone—including herself—to be grateful for everything they *did* have. Still, her pep talks were getting harder and harder to give, especially in the cold of winter.

It took a minute for Kim's eyes to adjust to the dimness of the shed. The air was thick with the smell of sweet hay mixed with a musty odor. Kim found the bag of carrots where she had tucked them a few days earlier, her private stash of treats to spoil the horses.

With carrot in hand, Kim walked slowly back to Lauren, passing the ranch's two miniature horse residents, Hope and Josie. The small mares—Hope a rich mahogany color and Josie with an almond-hued coat—had been donated by a loving owner who could no longer care for them. They had become instant favorites among the children. The commotion in the trailer had certainly gotten the miniature horses' attention too.

Speckles was still stomping his displeasure from his stall inside the trailer. Lauren was talking to him while leaning as far away from him as possible in the ten-foot-by-six-foot area.

"Mission accomplished," Kim called out, not wanting to surprise either of them. "Let's see if hunger will override his fear."

Lauren exited the trailer as Kim entered. She waved the carrot under Speckles' nose. His ears perked up as his lips greedily parted. Kim broke off a little chunk and fed it to him flat-handed. When Kim placed another chunk in her hand, she backed up a few steps, just out of the horse's reach. Enticed by the carrot, Speckles cautiously took two steps back. Kim fed him another carrot chunk and then clipped on a lead line.

"Back," she commanded, unconvinced the horse would obey, yet pleasantly surprised when he did.

"Just a few more steps." The moment Speckles was freed from the confines of the trailer, he began to calm down. Kim gave him a well-deserved back scratch.

"Here you go, boy," Kim said, watching him gobble down the last of the carrot. "That's much better, isn't it?"

Lauren tentatively approached the pair.

Kim motioned her closer.

"Thanks for the snack suggestion," she said, offering Speckles' lead line to Lauren. "It clearly worked."

After a brief hesitation followed by a hint of a smile, Lauren accepted the line and joined Kim in scratching the horse's side. Speckles accepted her touch, then began moving toward Joey. Two more curious onlookers raised their heads in a nearby field, a white pony named Shiloh and a chestnut mare named Essie.

Joey's ears flew forward and he took two steps back as Speckles approached. The two Appaloosas looked like twins from the back, differentiated only by the color of their spots—Joey's were black and Speckles' were brown. Kim, Lauren, and the group of volunteers held their collective breath as the two horses greeted one other.

Joey is your friend from the trailer, Speckles. You've both traveled a long way to get here. In her mind, Kim willed everything to go smoothly, knowing that oftentimes, introductions between horses can lead to rearing, kicking, or even biting. Given Speckles' earlier reaction, Kim was concerned for Joey.

"Barb, be ready to move Joey back if necessary," Kim instructed, grateful for her friend's natural giftedness with horses. Then, to the rest of the team, she added, "Let's just give the horses a minute to adjust and see how it goes."

Please, God, let this go smoothly, she silently prayed.

Lauren held Speckles' line loosely. As Kim turned to take the line from her, the horse lunged at Joey, teeth bared. Lauren held fast to the line, her eyes wide and fixed on Speckles. Joey and Barb didn't move as Speckles reared up. Lauren instinctively tightened her grip, trying to keep the line from being jerked out of her hand. Joey's head shot up, but he still didn't move. Speckles wasn't done, letting out a long whinny to proclaim his dominance. Joey took a step back, answering with a whinny of his own. Satisfied with Joey's seeming submission, Speckles abruptly ended the greeting and started to pick at the grass.

Everyone was relieved. After letting the horses spend a few minutes peacefully grazing, Kim looked at Lauren and Barb. "All right, guys. Let's get these boys into paddock two." Paddock two, a large rectangular-shaped field, was adjacent to Shiloh and Essie's pasture. It stretched from the edge of the common area to where it paralleled Highway 50. Each of the four fields on the ranch was cordoned off with flexible slat fencing topped by electrified wire.

Within the paddock, there was a three-sided wooden run-in shelter, a deep, black rubber water trough, and a wooden feedbox. Several trees—oaks, sweet gum, and a maple—stood at attention toward the back of the field, providing a canopy of shade in the summer.

Kim opened the gate, motioning Lauren to lead Speckles in first. Barb followed with Joey. Once everyone was inside, Lauren and Speckles headed left to the feedbox, while Barb and Joey lingered along the front perimeter by the water trough. After a few minutes, the two volunteers removed their respective horses' halter, giving the newest angels the run of their new home.

"Will they be okay?" Lauren asked Kim as they watched the two horses silently graze.

"They'll be just fine," she said. But truthfully? She had no idea. *Lord, please let them be okay*, she silently pleaded, suddenly wishing they were able to afford an overnight caretaker. She would sleep so much better knowing someone was watching over Joey to make sure he didn't fall, or trip, or get attacked by Speckles. Normally, she would not put two horses together right away, but they seemed to be getting along relatively well, and Tom had said it was important for Joey to have a companion.

The sun was dipping below the tree line when Kim walked the volunteers back to the parking lot, thanking them for being there to help with the unloading. As the small welcome committee dispersed, Barb hugged Kim, saying they should both go home, take a long, hot shower, and get a good night's rest.

"I will," Kim assured her. "I just want to check on Joey one more time."

Kim slowly made her way back to paddock two, taking in the peaceful atmosphere of the ranch. Horses lingered over hay boxes; others grazed on winter grass. As the wind picked up, Kim pulled her hat down lower. The air definitely had a cold bite to it. A hot shower suddenly sounded like heaven. But first, she needed to make sure Joey was okay.

Kim stood outside the fence. Speckles was near the hay box, his ears moving like a sonar device, his eyes wide and searching.

Well, he sure seems to have calmed down, Kim mused. Then she turned to watch Joey. He was still by the water trough. *Has he moved at all since I left him thirty minutes ago?* Then it hit her again. Suddenly, she saw the ranch with fresh eyes—Joey's eyes.

Eyes that couldn't see.

How was this going to work? How was he going to find his way to the hay box? To the shelter? *What was I thinking?*

Everyone trusted her to make wise decisions. They believed this would all work out because she said it would. But now, staring at a horse who couldn't see her, she suddenly felt overwhelmed.

Trust and worry. Worry and trust. Kim closed her eyes. In her mind, she could still see the pasture, the feedbox, the water trough, the woods, the fence—all the things Joey couldn't see.

Kim opened her eyes. She would have to show him.

"Don't worry, Joey," Kim called out. "I'll be right back."

The ranch was quickly becoming cloaked in the darkness of twilight, so she didn't have a lot of time. Kim ran to the tack shed to grab Joey's halter and lead line. *I have to help him get his bearings.*

"Here you go, boy," she said. "We're going to go for a little walk." Tugging gently, Kim led Joey away from the water trough and toward the gate.

"That's the gate," she explained. "That's where you will come in and out." She then turned left at the gate and walked the fence line with Joey toward the back of the field. She knew it was silly. Joey couldn't see or understand what she was saying. But it didn't matter. She needed to do something, needed to try to help him "see."

"Over there, on the other side of the fence, are Shiloh and Essie," she said, pointing toward the curious equines, watching from their pasture. "They will be nice neighbors."

When they reached the back of the field, Joey's ears flicked in the direction of the highway.

"Those are just cars," Kim reassured him. "They're noisy, but they won't hurt you. As long as you stay inside this fence, you'll be fine." Kim suddenly wondered if Joey had ever been close to a busy road before. Would the nearby traffic frighten him?

He seemed okay. "Maybe you should keep a safe distance from the fence for now," Kim cautioned. Then she began counting the steps from the back of the field toward the oak tree in the center of the paddock.

Fifty.

"Fifty steps to the tree, Joey," she said. Then she headed back to the water trough. "And one hundred steps to the water trough." Off in the distance, a horse whinnied. It was Spirit, a gorgeous buckskin gelding with an ebony mane and tail. "Oh, that's Spirit over there," she explained. "He's a good horse, although sometimes he can be a little grumpy. But he'll be a good neighbor too."

Was any of this helping? She wasn't convinced that it was, but frankly, she didn't know what else to do. And so she continued to give Joey the grand tour of paddock two, stopping every couple of yards for him to pull at the grass.

Speckles, keeping a close eye on the pair, had wandered over to the other side of the paddock to introduce himself to Shiloh and Essie over the fence.

Kim couldn't shake the fear that Joey wasn't going to be able to adjust. She chastised herself. *I don't know how to take care of a blind horse.* All the phone calls in the world with Tom, all the online articles and vet conversations couldn't have prepared her for this moment—standing face-to-face with the blind horse she was now responsible for. In many ways, she was as blind as Joey.

As she unfastened his halter, she prayed out loud. "Lord, I truly believed that you wanted Joey here. But now . . . it all feels too hard. Too frightening. Lord, you're going to have to see us all through this." Joey's nose touched her shoulder. Kim reached up and stroked the velvety spotted muzzle. "Please, God, take care of Joey. Please keep him safe."

She paused for a moment, waiting for a flood of peace to overtake her, or for some kind of sign or reassurance to appear from above. But the only thing that pierced the silence was Speckles whinnying in the distance.

Worry and trust, she thought. *You've done plenty of worrying. Now it's time to trust.*

Kim gave Joey's nose one more stroke.

"You've had a long day, Joey," she said. "Get some sleep, and I'll see you tomorrow. Good night, Speckles," she called out to the other Appaloosa, still standing at Shiloh and Essie's fence. "Look after Joey tonight, okay?"

Kim lingered at the gate for a few minutes more, watching as Joey and Speckles were enveloped by the darkness. Another gust of wind made her pull her collar tight around her neck as she turned and headed back toward the parking lot.

CHAPTER 4

SARAH STEWART WAS the first to arrive at the ranch the next morning, a half hour early for her shift. Being the newest feeding volunteer, the twenty-eight-year-old wanted to make sure she had plenty of time before the others arrived to review everything she had learned during her training the week before.

Hearing soft nickers coming from different pastures made Sarah smile. It had been a long time since she had been around horses—too long. She stood near an oak tree that had shed its leaves months earlier, and breathed in deeply. The crisp air enhanced the scent of sweet hay and horse manure wafting in her direction. Many people found the smell of manure unpleasant, but for her, it was the smell of love and safety. It was the smell of home.

A gust of wind whipped her ponytail into her face. She pulled her gray cap lower over her ears and tucked her hair into her jacket. The temperature hovered around forty degrees, but the wind made it feel much colder. Suddenly regretting her decision to be at the ranch so early, she decided to go to the feed shed to get out of the wind.

The building was locked. Sarah had forgotten to get the combination from PJ, the woman who had been training her. *Well, it's either back to the car, where I can crank up the heat, or take a fast-paced walk around the property.* She opted for a walk. *Gotta get my steps in before I need to leave for my paying job.*

While Sarah had never seen herself working as a receptionist at a dermatologist's office, it was the only job she had been able to get when she moved to Raleigh eight months ago. It might not have been her dream job, but it paid the bills and she liked her coworkers. And the later start time allowed her to spend mornings volunteering at Hope Reins, the one place she could be around the animals she loved most in this world—the only ones who had never betrayed her.

Sarah headed to Hope and Josie's enclosure. The diminutive pair trotted eagerly to her, then began clamoring for her attention by pushing each other out of the way, anxious to receive breakfast. She patted each one over the low fencing.

"Sorry, you two; just a little longer. It's coming," she assured them.

She left the two minis and walked at a brisk pace along the fence line. Horses beckoned her to stop with enchanting nickers and gentle stomps. But when they realized that Sarah had neither hay nor treats, the equine welcoming crew pulled their heads back one by one.

Sarah glanced at her phone. *Fifteen minutes before the rest of the team arrives. Must keep moving.*

She slowed when she came to paddock two. The field had

been empty the last time she was at the ranch, but now two horses were there. *That's right! Yesterday Kim went to pick up new horses.* Sarah stood watching the two Appaloosas from a distance. They looked so similar and yet so different.

Sarah remembered Kim mentioning that the one named Speckles had a brown head and a white-and-brown body. He was standing by the hay box—toward the front of the enclosure. When he turned his black almond-shaped eyes in her direction, his look seemed menacing. As she studied him, he bobbed and thrashed his head in an intimidating display. *With a name like Speckles, I thought he would be sweet, gentle, and easygoing.* The horse, snorting and stomping in front of her, was anything but.

In the middle of the field, the other horse was standing perfectly still as if he were sleeping. *Joey, the blind one. If only humans could sleep like that!* she marveled.

Sarah continued on, passing the next field shared by the buckskin Spirit and Gabe the Shetland pony. Gabe was one of her favorites; she loved the party pony's huge personality.

Checking her phone again, Sarah noted the time. The others would be arriving any minute now, so she began retracing her path back to the parking lot.

As she came upon paddock two, she noticed that Speckles was now grazing near the fence at the far end of the pasture. But Joey was still in the same spot in the middle of the field.

Sarah's stomach suddenly tightened.

He should be moving. Grazing.

Something felt wrong.

Sarah was slightly nervous about being in the same field as Speckles, but she needed to investigate Joey's odd behavior. When she opened the gate, Speckles raised his head at the sound of the metal latch opening and closing, his ears tracking her every move. Thankfully, he stayed where he was at the back of the field. Sarah slowly walked toward Joey, softly calling out his name to avoid startling the resting horse.

"Hey, Joey," she said. "You awake?"

And then she saw them—numerous superficial cuts and scratches, and a deep, bloody gash on his thigh. The cuts and scratches covered his legs, and the ragged four-inch gash seemed to take up his entire right thigh. His ears were up, but he gave no indication of even hearing the volunteer.

What happened here? Sarah surveyed the enclosed field. Everything looked normal; everything was where it should be. Sarah glared in Speckles' direction. *Did you have anything to do with this?* Without thinking, she reached out to touch the injured horse, but caught herself and pulled back, fearful that her touch would cause more distress than comfort. Sarah kept scanning the surroundings. And then . . . she noticed something.

Toward the back corner of the paddock, where one side fence connected to the back fence, several slats hung askew. When she ran over to investigate, Sarah found a tangled mess of electric wire fencing broken and jumbled up on the ground. In a split second, everything became painfully clear. *Joey must have run into the fencing and gotten tangled in the wire.*

Sarah's stomach lurched. The broken wire stuck out like lethal spikes—spikes that would have repeatedly pierced Joey's skin as he became more and more terrified. She sprinted back to him, peeling off her coat as she ran. She balled up the garment and threw it toward the gate before slowly approaching the statue-like horse, gently extending her hand to let him know that he was not alone.

"Oh, buddy," she whispered, "I'm so sorry." The sight of his open flesh wound made her slightly woozy even though she had treated many wounds when she had been on an equine health and wellness team years before. She looked away momentarily and concentrated on slowing her breathing. "I'm so sorry you got hurt."

Joey's ears flicked ever so slightly, and his tail swished—twice. Sarah's heart leaped at the reaction.

She pieced together the likely scenario from the injuries and the evidence on the ground. It was obvious that once tangled, Joey had tried to break free. And while he did indeed break free, the wire put up quite a fight. As Sarah imagined him thrashing about in the dangerous wire, she got sick to her stomach. No wonder he didn't want to risk moving again.

Sarah held her hand in front of Joey's nostrils, cautiously touching his nose. The horse released a forceful breath before pressing his muzzle ever so lightly into her hand.

A sense of protectiveness like she had never felt before welled up inside her. "You're safe now, Joey," she whispered, leaning into him. "You're safe."

Unsure of what to do next, Sarah stood with the horse for several minutes, stroking his nose and talking softly to him. The adrenaline that had powered her sprint across the field slowly dissipated, and a chill shook her body. Sarah left Joey's side just long enough to retrieve her coat from the ground where she had tossed it. She zipped it up and thrust her hands deep into the pockets to warm them up.

"All right, big guy. The others will be here soon, and they'll know what to do. But how about a little walk for now?"

Just then, she heard a car door slam in the distance. "Oh,

thank God!" she said out loud. The other feeding volunteers were arriving.

"Joey," she said, with a feigned lightness to her voice, "wanna follow me?" Sarah clucked her tongue, and Joey took one step forward. "There you go, Joey. Good job. Nice and slow."

The horse took another step, and blood oozed from the cuts on his legs. *What was I thinking? I probably made it all worse.* "I'm sorry, buddy. I'm sorry."

"Good morning, Sarah!" PJ's cheerful voice came from the direction of the parking lot.

Sarah tried her best to keep her voice calm as she replied, "PJ, Joey's been hurt."

PJ, who was short in stature but large in personality, darted toward paddock two, squeezing herself through the fence slats. She raced over to Sarah and Joey and gasped when she saw the wounds.

"What happened?"

Sarah pointed to the back fence and explained her theory. The entire time she talked, she kept her left hand resting lightly on Joey's side to stay physically connected to the animal. It seemed to be working. After a few minutes, Sarah felt Joey's body relax ever so slightly.

PJ pulled out her cell phone to let Kim know what had happened. Sarah stayed with Joey, talking to him and trying her best to keep him calm. He shifted his weight back and forth between his injured back legs, and kept craning his head toward the gash on his thigh. Unable to reach the source of pain, he leaned his side into Sarah. She stood firm against his weight, wishing that she could make the pain go away.

"Kim is calling the vet and is on her way here," PJ said, crouching down to assess the injuries.

Joey pawed at the ground.

"Are you okay to stay with Joey for a few minutes while I go tell the others what's going on, and they can start feeding?" Sarah nodded as PJ jogged away.

"I gotcha, boy," Sarah said, tracing a large black spot on his side. The plum-sized spot tapered at the end, making it look like a large raindrop. "You're gonna be okay," she whispered into his neck. "I'm not going to leave you."

Ten minutes later, PJ was back. She reached into her pocket and pulled out a large carrot, breaking it into thirds. Joey eagerly took the treat and seemed to be coming out of his trancelike state. *How long was he standing here?* Sarah wondered. He had acted on his natural instinct to run from a dangerous situation, and that had freed him from the electric wire, but at a painful cost. So he froze where he thought he was safe from further harm. She watched Joey take a tiny step toward PJ in trust.

Before too long, Sarah saw Kim's car pull up, followed by another vehicle. *It must be the vet.*

"Is he okay? What happened?" Kim asked as she threw open the gate, with Dr. Ryan Gallagher a few steps behind her. Sarah pointed to the pile of mangled wire in the back corner of the pasture.

"Oh no, I didn't even think about that," Kim moaned. "How could I have missed that?"

Relieved to have others more capable than herself tending to Joey, Sarah stepped away, opening up space for the vet to inspect the injured horse.

Dr. Gallagher, a recent graduate from the North Carolina State University College of Veterinary Medicine, practiced at the veterinarian hospital on campus. He and Kim had met one day when they were walking their respective dogs in the neighborhood. As they talked, the two of them discovered a shared love of horses. When Kim mentioned what she was doing at Hope Reins, Dr. Gallagher generously offered his services.

He had been their go-to vet ever since—a double blessing because of his proximity to the ranch and his obvious love of animals. However, Kim soon discovered that keeping horses healthy was not cheap. When they had to take Essie to the animal hospital for the first time, Kim walked out owing $1,700.

Here in the pasture, Dr. Gallagher slowly circled Joey, inspecting each cut and abrasion. From his bag he pulled out a bottle of saline, a handful of sterile packed dressings, a tube of antiseptic, and a roll of self-sticking gauze. After carefully putting a halter over Joey's head, the vet clipped on a leather line and handed the end to Sarah.

"Just hang on to him for me," he said. "This might get a bit of a reaction from him," he added with a wink. His quiet confidence put Sarah at ease. Kneeling beside the horse, Dr. Gallagher began cleaning Joey's wounds. The vet was right— Joey did react, raising his legs and attempting to move away. Joey's sudden movement, combined with the human activity inside the pasture, agitated Speckles, who was now pacing along the east fence line. Sarah held Joey's line firmly.

"Easy, Joey. The doctor is just trying to help you," she said softly to the distressed horse. "It'll be over soon."

Dr. Gallagher wrapped Joey's back left leg in gauze, which was tricky to do with a stomping target. "This leg definitely took the brunt of the damage. Nothing too deep, but we want to guard against any infection." When he finished, he stood up and thoroughly flushed the large gash on Joey's thigh before applying a generous amount of ointment. "The laceration should begin to scab over quickly. Keep flushing it with saline a few times a day and applying this ointment, and it should heal without any trouble."

Seeing Kim's concern, he patted Joey's rump. "He should be just fine. Thankfully, most of the abrasions are superficial. He was actually pretty lucky. It could have been much worse."

"I just can't believe I didn't think about the wire fencing," Kim said, still frustrated from her lack of foresight. "We talked about moving obstacles from the paddock, but the fencing never occurred to me. It just never crossed my mind . . ."

"We discussed this, Kim, remember?" he said. "You cannot possibly plan for every situation that will come up with Joey. His blindness will continue to present challenges. In fact, there will be times that you are caring for him when you will feel like it's 'the blind leading the blind.' But you *will* figure it out."

Dr. Gallagher removed Joey's halter and unhooked the lead line, putting the objects in his bag. "You have my number, Kim. Call me anytime. If I'm with another patient, then leave me a message, and I'll get back to you. But I promise, you've got this."

"Ryan, I—we," she clarified, looking at the team of volunteers around her, "we cannot thank you enough for coming out this morning to treat Joey. And thank you for answering all my questions the past few weeks. Your belief in us means a lot."

Sarah overheard Kim ask the vet what she owed him as they walked from the paddock. Sarah couldn't hear his reply, but a shake of his head, followed by a hug from Kim, made it pretty clear what the answer was.

Joey's nicker got Sarah's attention. He was shifting his weight and stomping his back leg. Then he took a step forward, bobbing his head up and down.

Across the field, Speckles was clearly making his presence known, whinnying, bobbing his head, and stomping the ground. *I completely forgot about Speckles.* Joey's ears turned toward his pasture-mate standing about thirty feet away, and the blind horse began walking in the direction of the sound. Speckles' dark eyes followed his every move. After several steps, Joey halted, craning his head back toward his leg, trying to reach the gash on his thigh.

Speckles whinnied again, and Joey's attention was refocused on the other horse's location, leading Joey right to him. Joey now stood just a few feet from Speckles. Sarah balled her hands up in her pockets, wishing she were still holding Joey's lead line. *What if Speckles tries to bite or kick him?*

Joey took another step forward and bumped his head into Speckles' neck. Sarah, who had been following Joey from a safe distance, bit her bottom lip. *Here it comes. Joey has violated Speckles' personal space.*

But to Sarah's amazement, there was no reaction from Speckles. No angry thrashing. No biting. No kicking. Instead, Speckles took a step back before letting out a forceful snort. Joey responded by raising and lowering his head as if whole-heartedly agreeing to something Speckles said.

Sarah stood riveted as Speckles walked several feet away before stopping and nickering. Joey's ears flew forward, and he answered with a low-pitched neigh. Sarah started toward him, but Speckles stomped his foot and snorted again, causing her to freeze in her tracks. Joey walked right to Speckles and placed his head on Speckles' shoulder. Speckles mirrored the motion, resting his head on Joey's shoulder in what appeared to be an equine embrace. The two stood together, nuzzling each other, for several minutes.

Sarah could hardly believe her eyes. *What is happening? Who is this gentle, docile horse nuzzling Joey?* It almost looked as though Speckles were trying to comfort Joey instead of shunning him—inviting him closer, as if he understood that Joey was hurt and that he couldn't see.

By nature, horses are pack animals, driven by instinct, hierarchy, and dominance. Weaker members of the herd are treated as such, seen as a liability and often attacked. But Speckles was doing no such thing. Instead, he was literally reaching out to Joey. It was fascinating to watch. Sarah, deciding that it was safe to leave the two horses alone, made her way to the front of the field, where PJ was filling up the water trough.

After a few minutes of peaceful companionship, Speckles walked to the feedbox full of fresh hay and began eating. A moment later, Joey joined his new friend there.

Yet, when Joey began to lower his head into the box, Speckles lunged at him—neck outstretched and front hooves slamming the ground, letting loose an ear-piercing warning. Joey, not the least bit deterred by his injuries, shot off away from the hay box as if it were on fire. Tail low and ears flat, he made his way to the place where Sarah had first found him. Every time Speckles raised his head from the hay box, he looked at Joey. *Stay away.*

"Well, that's gonna be a problem," PJ said to Sarah.

Sarah nodded. Feeling the need to reassure Joey that everything was going to be okay after Speckles' bizarre Jekyll-and-Hyde behavior, Sarah pulled a generous handful of hay from a bale just outside the paddock and walked over to the quietly grazing horse.

"Well, buddy," she said, "it looks like your new friend is fine with nuzzling but isn't much for sharing, huh?" She rubbed his chin. "One thing at a time, I guess, right? One thing at a time."

CHAPTER 5

KIM STOOD WITH a small group of trainers and feeding volunteers outside Joey's paddock, her fingers on her temples, pushing against a tension headache. The pressure had started the moment she answered her phone and heard about Joey's accident. She squeezed her eyes against the throbbing pain. Joey's first night at Hope Reins had been a disaster. She had promised to protect him and yet had traumatized him instead.

"Kim, are you okay?" The concern in Barb's voice made Kim open her eyes.

"Yes, sorry," Kim replied with as much of a smile as she could muster. "Just a bad headache." As she ran her fingers through her hair, she continued. "I am sick about this. I should have thought about the electric fencing—but thank God I had forgotten to turn it on!" she said, suddenly realizing how much worse Joey's injuries could have been if the wire had been hot.

"Kim, you had no way of knowing this would happen," Barb shot back. "This was not your fault. You've given that horse a home—a second chance. This accident could have happened just as easily to a seeing horse."

Everyone encircling her nodded in agreement. Too choked up to speak, Kim mouthed the words *Thank you.*

These people had quickly become like family. When she decided to follow God's call and start the ranch, she knew she would be caring for horses and—hopefully—helping people. But she had no idea that she would be receiving so much—so much love, so much encouragement.

Kim glanced across paddock two and saw Sarah standing halfway between Joey and the gate. She waved Sarah over.

Kim had only talked with Sarah twice. In fact, the first time she met her was the day Tom had called about Joey. Sarah had come to the ranch that day looking for somewhere to volunteer. She had seemed so nervous. It all made sense when Sarah confessed to Kim that she had already reached out to six other ranches, all for-profit riding barns, who had dismissed her offer to volunteer her time, either claiming that they had enough help already or simply never calling her back. Kim couldn't imagine turning away willing help. She had eagerly welcomed Sarah.

Kim forced her attention back to the pressing issue at hand: Joey's safety.

"Barb is right," Kim said, determined to be the leader this group deserved. "We are not going to sit around blaming ourselves. Joey got hurt, and we all hate that. So let's channel our energy into forming a plan to prevent this from happening again."

The speech was as much for herself as anyone. The group immediately began firing ideas.

"What if we build an enclosed stall for Joey?" Jo Anne asked.

"Maybe we move him to the big field?" Barb suggested.

"I've heard that sometimes having a goat in with a blind horse is helpful," Sarah said.

"Or," Jo Anne said, "we could take the electric wire fencing down."

"What about creating a barrier in front of the wire?" Barb added.

All good ideas, but none would solve the immediate problem of ensuring Joey's safety this moment. And none that would help him learn the boundaries of his field for the future. Suddenly, Sarah's phone dinged, signaling an incoming e-mail. Everyone looked in her direction.

"Sorry 'bout that," Sarah said, reaching in her pocket to silence her phone.

"That's it!" Barb shouted. "What about chimes?"

Barb explained the idea. "If we hang wind chimes around his fencing, maybe he'll realize there's a boundary there and he won't walk into the wire again."

Kim thought about it for a moment. *Could that actually work?* It made sense—at least in theory. Joey needed to *hear* his boundary markers. And it was something that could be implemented *today*. Anxious to try anything, Kim said, "Okay, wind chimes it is! How many do you think we'll need?"

"As many as possible," Jo Anne said. "We can attach them to the fence posts all along the perimeter, and maybe even hang some from the trees." She gestured toward the wooded area.

"Good idea," said Kim, genuinely smiling for the first time that morning. "All right, ladies—we're off to Walmart!"

As Barb, Jo Anne, and Sarah headed for the parking lot, Kim flagged down Jo Anne's husband, Hank, who had become their all-around handyman. She pulled him aside and asked if he could try to repair the wire fencing that Joey had gotten tangled up in.

"Make sure you wear heavy work gloves," she cautioned, nodding in Joey's direction. "That stuff is razor sharp."

Hank gave her a wink, gently implying he was more than capable of handling the wire and yet too much of a gentleman to tell her so.

Truth be told, Kim wished they didn't need the electric fencing at all. But the flexible PVC alternative fencing they had was too flimsy to keep the horses safely confined on the property. And with twenty rolling acres to enclose, who could possibly afford *that* much wooden fencing?

Worry and trust. "I *need* to get better at the second half of that," Kim scolded herself quietly as she headed to her car.

———

At Walmart, the four women quickly discovered that the middle of February is not the optimal time to shop for wind chimes. So after grabbing the entire, albeit meager, supply, they continued to make the rounds of every lawn and garden store in a ten-mile radius until the trunk of Kim's car was full. The ride home was quite musical, each bump and turn producing a cacophony of jingles and clangs.

There was an eclectic mix of traditional and whimsical designs: round wooden tops with long metal tubes; dainty chimes featuring butterflies on clear wire; repurposed kitchen utensils; animal cutouts; and even rainbow-colored swirls—close to forty chimes in all.

After stopping for a quick bite to eat at a local deli, they headed back to the ranch with the booty.

"How should we hang these?" Jo Anne asked Kim as they unloaded the wind chimes into a wheelbarrow.

"Let's use bailing twine to tie them to each fence post."

"Sounds like a plan."

Kim headed to the office to grab the twine. A thick blanket of clouds was moving in, quickly turning the sky gray. Spring could not arrive soon enough for her. After scouring the small room and rummaging through all the bins, she finally found several rolls of jute twine left over from their grand opening event, just over six months ago.

The newly finished ranch had had such a festive feel that day. Kim had been surprised that so many people had come out to explore the ranch. But, then again, it was a free event with an open invitation to come and meet the horses, which was a big draw for families with young children. Overall, the event had been a success, generating several referrals and many donations.

We might have to do that again sometime, Kim thought, tossing the rolls of twine into an old water bucket. *Soon.*

As Kim approached paddock two, she heard a soft but distinct and steady clicking sound. It was if someone far away were banging a wooden spoon against a pot. *Where is that coming from?* She called out to Hank, who was repairing the wire fencing. Although he couldn't hear her, Hank headed her way with Joey following close behind. The closer Hank got, the louder the clicking became.

"Hank, I think your pants are clicking!" Kim said, laughing.

Hank looked at her sheepishly. "That they are, I suppose," he said, pulling his phone from his back pocket and pausing the sound. "I didn't want ol' Joey to bump into me while I was fixing the fence. I figured if he could hear me, he would know where I was. Same idea as the wind chimes, I suppose. A while back, my granddaughter downloaded a metronome program on my phone to use when she practices the piano at our house. It makes a steady beat, so I thought it might work for Joey."

"You're a genius, Hank! We are so blessed to have you working with us."

Hank patted Joey's neck. "Joey likes the clicking, so I predict he'll respond well to the wind chimes, too."

"Thank you, Hank." Kim smiled as the older gentleman made his way back to the office, and a rush of gratitude flowed over her. *I have incredible people helping me.* "Are you ready to hang some wind chimes, ladies?"

As soon as Jo Anne pulled the first set of wind chimes out of the wheelbarrow and handed them to Sarah, Joey's ears flicked and twitched inquisitively.

Speckles was standing near the gate when the women entered the paddock. He turned his backside to them and Joey, seemingly indifferent to the clanging intrusion. But as the volunteers began untangling the chimes, Speckles whinnied his concern and took several steps back. Kim noticed Sarah tensing up in response to Speckles' reaction.

"What's Speckles' story?" Sarah asked, keeping a close eye on the unpredictable horse as the group of women made their way further into the field.

"The person from Equine Rescue League told us that Speckles was purchased by breeders in Virginia who were looking for Appaloosas. He was kept in a stall and only taken out for breeding with no real turn-out time. No time to run around and just be a horse. I guess the owners didn't want to risk anything happening to their top stallion," Kim said.

"After a while, the operation started to lose money, and the owners began to let things go. Apparently someone affiliated with the farm became concerned about how some of the horses were being treated and called animal control. They found several starving and neglected horses. Poor Speckles was found in a dark stall, standing knee deep in his own muck. His ribs were protruding so much that they feared they would break during transport, and his feet were a putrid mess from being in the muck for so long."

Sarah flinched at the description, imagining how much distress Speckles had endured.

Kim went on. "After animal control picked him up, he went to a foster ranch where they treated his wounds, got his hooves healthy, and put some weight on him. They also had him gelded. We visited him twice to make sure he would fit in at Hope Reins. He appeared calm and compliant both times, although we were warned that he was unintelligent and stubborn. All we saw was a horse in need of a home, nothing else— nothing like he's been the past twenty-four hours."

Kim's voice got quieter. "I'm starting to worry that I might have seen what I wanted to see. I just wanted so badly to give him a second chance, give him a future. Show him that there's more to life than being used like that."

"Poor thing," Sarah said, looking at the horse with new understanding. "That's horrible. I can see why you wanted him. Maybe he just needs time to adjust."

Kim hoped Sarah was right. Speckles *would* need time to adjust. He'd been through a lot in the past six months. He had to be disoriented and frightened.

As if knowing they had been talking about him, Speckles, standing just ten feet away from the group, erupted in a high-pitched whinny. Joey wheeled and trotted over to him, his ears up and his head tilted toward the agitated horse.

Speckles unleashed another earsplitting cry and looked as if he were about to flee. Instinctively, Kim backed away. Joey took a step forward.

"Easy, big guy," Kim reassured him. "No one is going to hurt you—especially not these chimes. We just have to give you some time to get used to them." Kim glanced at Sarah and tried to smile reassuringly.

"Absolutely," Sarah said. "I'll start hanging them on the far side of the paddock."

Kim turned her attention back to Speckles. "These are just to help Joey out," she said calmly. "Wanna see one?" She stretched her arm out, a whimsical frog with lily pad chimes dangling from her hand. Speckles eyed the unusual instrument. He stood motionless for several minutes as Kim urged him forward. Finally, curiosity won out. Standing before Kim, Speckles lowered his head and bumped the wind chime, sending the lily pads dancing. Speckles immediately jerked his head back and stomped his front hooves.

"Easy, boy." Kim spoke quietly while holding out the chimes again for the horse to continue investigating. Speckles did have an intimidating look about him, but the truth was, this horse needed them. Kim was determined to give him a better life.

"It's okay, Speckles, come on over and—" Kim jumped as Joey suddenly appeared in her peripheral vision, lured by the chimes. The blind horse showed no fear as he made a beeline to Kim and bumped the chimes with his nose to make them jingle. Speckles suddenly lost interest in the new object and turned away to graze.

"Thanks for the assist, Joey," Kim chuckled, patting the horse with her free hand.

Satisfied that the horses were comfortable, Sarah, Barb, Jo Anne, and Kim got to work hanging chimes at each fence post and on each of the trees located in the middle of the paddock. *Surely Joey won't walk into a tree, but it's better to be safe than sorry.*

Just over an hour after they had begun, the four women stood back to admire their handiwork. The chimes looked surprisingly beautiful, and their wind-generated sounds created a cheery atmosphere in an otherwise dreary day. Other than the occasional sniff from Joey and a curious nibble or two from Speckles, the horses left the tingling chimes alone.

"Ladies, we did it," Kim said, placing her arms around Jo Anne's and Barb's shoulders. "Thank you so much for your help."

"I think it looks really good. Very chic." Jo Anne nodded her approval.

As long as they do the job, Kim thought. The chimes would be pointless if they didn't keep Joey away from the fencing.

"I'm going to grab a halter and walk Joey around the fence line," Kim said. "He needs to know what these chimes are for."

"Good idea," Sarah said.

Kim stopped at the first chime and encouraged Joey to bump it. They repeated the same process at every chime along the fence and at each tree. Joey's head bobbed, his tail and ears relaxed. Sporadically, Joey would nicker and Speckles would nicker in response, almost as if they were playing a game of Marco Polo.

The second time around the enclosure, Kim stopped Joey at every third chime before walking him toward the site of his accident—a location she had avoided the first time around.

Hank had already repaired the fencing. It looked as if nothing had ever happened. Yet a glance at Joey's bandaged legs brought the painful reality right back to the forefront of Kim's mind.

As they paused momentarily, Joey made a low blowing sound, the air reverberating through his large nostrils in a staccato rhythm. His ears flicked and turned as if searching for something. Within seconds, Speckles let out a loud deep sigh. Joey turned his head toward him and relaxed his ears.

"Are you two talking to each other?" Kim asked, looking from one horse to the other.

Joey and Kim arrived at the gate again. Kim was about to start a third go-around when Barb stopped her.

"Joey's got it. Let's give him a break and let him investigate on his own."

But did he have it? Surely he needed another pass.

"Sweetie, he's tired. You're tired. Let's leave this one in God's hands for now, okay? It's only two o'clock. You can sit in the office and watch him through the window."

Reluctantly, Kim unfastened Joey's halter and turned him loose.

Worry and trust, she thought. Then she corrected herself. *No. Just trust.*

CHAPTER 6

"No sir!" Lauren hollered at Speckles, seeing him charge Joey again at the hay bin. She had been there the day Speckles arrived, when he nearly bit Kim's hand, and without really thinking, she hopped through the fence rails and into the paddock, finger wagging.

As she stood with her index finger a foot from the jaws of a bullying horse, she began to have second thoughts. *What is this going to accomplish exactly?*

The two Appaloosas had been at Hope Reins for almost a week, and though the wind chimes had effectively kept Joey from running into the electric wire fence, they did not protect him from Speckles, who still charged Joey at every feeding time, refusing to let him near the hay box. The volunteers had started leaving Joey's hay on the ground near the gate, but Lauren wasn't keen on that solution. She couldn't imagine forcing one of her two daughters to eat off the floor because the other one kept pushing her away from the table.

So every day, Lauren pulled four flakes—smaller sections of hay—from the large bale in the feed shed and carried them to the feedbox in the middle of paddock two. Then she pushed the wheelbarrow containing the rest of the herd's hay back through the paddock gate and stood outside the fence to watch what would happen next.

Right on cue, Speckles sauntered to the box. At first, Joey seemed uninterested in breakfast. But soon, Speckles' chomping got his pasture-mate's attention, and Joey began to cautiously move forward. His head bobbed as he walked, his jaw moving as if chewing on an invisible stalk of hay. Lauren quickly noticed that Speckles was glaring, his ears pinned back so far they touched his brown mane. He was a horse ready to strike. Poor Joey, unable to see the warning signs, was oblivious. *Maybe he thinks this time will be different,* Lauren reasoned. *Gotta give Joey credit for trying.*

Speckles was certainly creating a reputation for himself at Hope Reins—and it wasn't a good one. His propensity to kick and bite when upset was not winning him many friends at the ranch, either human or equine.

She had heard that Speckles had been sweet to Joey on the day they discovered his injuries, but since then, the staff had reported nothing but bully-like behavior. *It just doesn't make sense.*

The previous day, Barb's teenage daughter, Anna, a natural with horses, had volunteered to assess Speckles' ability to carry a rider—one of the many aspects of building a relationship with a child at Hope Reins. Speckles had stomped and snorted as Anna mounted him, but he seemed to settle down as she got adjusted in the saddle. However, the moment she had flicked the reins and clucked her tongue for him to walk, Speckles grew visibly agitated. Thinking he just needed a few more minutes to relax, Anna kept walking him, eventually signaling him to trot. A few steps later, Speckles bucked and Anna went flying off. Fortunately, she wasn't seriously hurt, but the incident was one more black mark against Speckles.

As Lauren watched Speckles, she wondered if the abuse he had endured at the breeding ranch had rendered him untrainable. She was beginning to feel sorry for the rescued horse. And then . . . Speckles attacked Joey once again, teeth nipping at the air—a bully and his victim.

Lauren had had enough. With one hand on her hip, she stood between the two horses, wagged her finger at Speckles, and yelled at the top of her lungs, "No, SIR! That is NOT how we treat our friends! You will not charge Joey anymore. Do you hear me?"

Speckles' nostrils flared as he flattened his ears.

Uh-oh, Lauren thought, losing a little of her bravado. Determined to show no fear, she took a single step forward. Speckles held his ground, snorting his displeasure. Lauren honed in on his eyes, staring the horse down as she moved in closer. He stomped his front right leg against the ground, sending bits of hay and dry grass into the air. Lauren took another step. Speckles' eyes twitched, and his muscles tightened. *One more step.* Lauren inhaled deeply, steadying herself for what might come. She should have turned back long ago, but now she was committed. She would see this through. She would . . .

Suddenly Speckles moved backward, his reaction nearly throwing Lauren off-balance. She stopped, not believing what had just happened. *I won.* Speckles had submitted to her. Granted, it was what she'd been hoping for, but she didn't actually think it would work. She studied his eyes again. They didn't appear to be filled with as much tension. He released a long sigh as he retreated another step. Then he tilted his head to the right, watching her.

"Good boy," Lauren whispered. "That wasn't so hard, was it?"

Emboldened by her victory, she extended her arm toward Speckles, offering her closed fist for his inspection. It took several seconds, but then Speckles bumped her fist with his nose, blowing a puff of air on it. They looked at each other again. That was when she saw it—the spark of intelligence. The twinkle of understanding. This horse was not dumb. No, this horse was smart. Very smart.

Granted, Lauren's horse experience was limited. However, she had grown up with dogs and competed in agility with them, a popular dog sport where the canine competitor is directed through a course of obstacles by its human partner. She knew what it took to train an animal. She knew that look—that "Teach me, I want to learn" look. Speckles' behavior was a challenging puzzle she wanted to solve.

Taking two more nonchalant steps toward Speckles, Lauren was inches from the horse. She gently touched a white spot on his cheek, then scratched behind his ear.

"Speckles, who are you *really*?" she asked.

Sensing that Speckles had stopped eating, Joey decided to get some breakfast. But as soon as Speckles heard Joey pulling hay from the box, his head whipped around. Lauren felt Speckles tense up—on alert again, and ready to attack.

"Oh no you don't," Lauren said, winding her fingers through his short brown mane. "You, my friend, are going to let Joey have a turn."

Lauren placed herself directly in front of Speckles. Every

time he moved, she moved, effectively blocking his path. Speckles pawed at the ground, his hooves digging grooves in the sparse grass. Lauren knew that he was gearing up to charge.

She wagged her finger in his face again. "No sir," she interjected, holding her arm out in front of him. "You stay right here."

Lauren began scratching Speckles' neck, giving Joey more time to finish.

"You're okay, Joey," Lauren assured him. "Speckles is going to share today."

Joey cautiously ate three more mouthfuls before quickly retreating. Clearly, he was not going to push his luck with Speckles.

"At least it's a start," Lauren muttered, trying to convince herself that Speckles could be a good pasture-mate for Joey—someday.

Lauren lowered her arm to release Speckles from his timeout. She patted the horse one more time before walking over to Joey and giving him a scratch on the rump.

"Don't let him boss you around."

Satisfied that all was well, Lauren left the paddock, pausing to massage her right knee. Lately, it seemed as if the ever-present dull pain were becoming more intense. Lauren braced herself against a weathered picnic table. She was trembling from the physical pain but also from the realization that Speckles could easily have kicked or bitten her. *What was I thinking?*

Sarah interrupted Lauren's thoughts. "That was pretty impressive—risky and incredibly dangerous, but impressive. I haven't seen that technique before, but it seemed effective, although probably not something Kim would have condoned."

"Yeah, I don't imagine wagging your finger in the face of an irritable horse is going to be in any horse training manuals,"

Lauren joked. "But sometimes the mom instincts just take over. Honestly, I think Speckles just needs to know what we expect from him, to learn his boundaries—just like Joey."

Sarah nodded. The Appaloosas were peacefully grazing several feet from the hay box where all the drama had taken place just minutes ago.

"The fact is," Lauren said, "I detected something in Speckles—a hint of understanding. I think he needs us to understand him. Does that make sense?" Lauren continued to rub her knee.

Sarah couldn't hide the sadness that suddenly swept over her. "Yes, I think it does."

The two women stood silently for a few moments before Sarah added, "Maybe Speckles needs us to understand how his past affects his present."

Of course! Lauren looked at Sarah with newfound respect as someone wise beyond her years. When they had first met, Lauren had thought Sarah seemed a bit standoffish. Lauren was fifteen years older than Sarah, and the extent of her athleticism was keeping up with her two children. She hadn't found much in common with the younger, fit volunteer. But now she was beginning to wonder if she had judged Sarah too quickly.

"That's exactly what I mean," Lauren answered, forcing her thoughts back to Speckles. "The food guarding and hoarding makes perfect sense. How does he know he'll get food each day, when he went so long without it at the other barn? Of course he wants to protect that food, and he sees every other horse as a threat."

Yes, Speckles needed to learn to trust them, to know that he could depend on them.

Both women watched the horses, all of them serenaded by the wind chimes swaying in the breeze.

Sarah finally realized it was time to call it a day. "I guess I should get back to the feed shed and make sure everything's put away."

"I'll walk with you."

"Oh no you won't," Sarah commanded teasingly. "People who stop a bullying horse are automatically exempt from cleanup duty."

Lauren smiled. "Deal," she said. Truthfully, she was grateful for the break. The pain in her knee was getting worse. She winced as she put weight on it, forcing herself to hobble a few steps to loosen the joint. She stopped to massage the knee some more, frustrated when the pain spread to her hand as well. Every day seemed to bring new pain to a different joint, and countless doctor visits had only raised more questions, not provided answers. Was it fibromyalgia? Arthritis? Bursitis? No two doctors seemed to agree.

She took a few tentative steps. The pain was finally lessening. Across the paddock, Speckles whinnied, snorted, and shook his head. Yes, Speckles had some issues, but Lauren was drawn to him, almost as if God had placed them both here at the same time for a reason.

As Lauren continued to walk off the pain, Joey let out a soft neigh. Immediately, Speckles called out with what sounded like a low rumble of laughter, directing Joey back to him.

A bully one moment and a best friend the next. "You are one complicated horse, Mr. Speckles."

———

Lauren wasn't on the schedule the next morning, but she came anyway—in time to intercept the hay for Speckles and Joey.

Maneuvering her way through the gate, she deposited her burden in the feedbox. Not surprisingly, Speckles was the first to arrive. He eyed Lauren as he lowered his head and tore into his breakfast. The moment Joey began moving toward him, Speckles lifted his head and snorted a warning.

"Oh no you don't, mister," Lauren corrected, extending her arms out from her sides to make herself look intimidating.

Speckles eyed her, assessing his options. But the moment Joey moved closer to the hay, Speckles started to lunge.

"No sir!" Lauren commanded sternly, holding her left arm in front of him.

She needed him to learn that he did not have to fight for his food, that they would give him all he needed. When she began to approach him, Speckles snorted, vigorously shook his head, and took a step back.

"Good boy!" she cheered, smiling widely. "Yes! That's good, Speckles."

Speckles' ears twitched forward, his tail swooshing behind him. *He knows I'm praising him. He knows he did good.* Of course, now came the real test. After several minutes with Joey eating and Speckles waiting, Lauren lowered her arm, signaling to the horse.

"Okay, Speckles, come and eat with Joey."

Speckles eyed Lauren momentarily before lowering his head. His brown head bumped Joey's, and Joey stopped mid-chew. But nothing happened. Speckles ignored Joey, and the two of them ate side by side.

Lauren practiced the same feeding routine with Speckles throughout the week. In just five days, Speckles had gone from breakfast bully to polite dining partner. The transformation had gotten the attention of everyone at the ranch, including Kim.

"What you have done with Speckles is amazing," Kim complimented Lauren one morning over a latte at Kim's favorite coffee shop.

"Thank you," Lauren said, still a little surprised that Kim had invited her to grab a cup of coffee after she had finished feeding the horses. She had been even more surprised that Kim was aware of her work with Speckles. After all, she did have an entire ministry to run.

"Lauren, I'm so glad for this chance to get to know you a little better," Kim started, smiling at her. "And to meet your girls." Lauren's two young daughters, seven-year-old Harper and ten-year-old Kate, shyly looked up from their schoolwork. "You've been volunteering with us for a few months, right? What brought you to Hope Reins?"

"Well, I had seen the Hope Reins sign when my husband and I were driving home from a birthday party, and then the following day Harper noticed a horse by the road and started pleading with me to stop so she could pet him." Lauren chuckled at the memory of Harper saying, "Mommy, I think that horse is lonely. Let's go say hi."

"So after a quick Google search, I discovered that Hope Reins was having a big opening event, and we decided to check it out. When the girls heard about the feeding teams, well, they pretty much signed me up. They love to run around while I take care of the horses, and—" she paused to wink at her girls—"all that exercise totally counts as PE credit for their homeschool program."

Kim laughed and leaned toward the girls, giving them high

fives. "Smart idea." Turning her attention back to Lauren, she asked, "How long have you been homeschooling?"

Lauren took a long sip of her unsweetened tea before answering. "Since Kate started kindergarten." She looked at her older daughter and smiled. "I had always liked the idea of homeschooling, especially the freedom I imagined it would bring. But then, the same year Kate turned five," she said sadly, "homeschooling became a necessity."

Lauren paused, measuring what she was about to say next.

"I began having pain, debilitating pain," she clarified. "What I thought was a twisted knee has turned into a five-year search for answers. With constant doctor visits, tests, and days when I can't get out of bed, we needed the flexibility of homeschooling." Lauren glanced at a worksheet Harper had just completed and gave her a thumbs-up. "I mean, I've lost count of how many times we've done homeschool at doctors' offices."

"I like doing homeschool at Hope Reins," Kate interjected, handing her paper to her mother for review and receiving a nod and a smile.

"Oh, Lauren, I had no idea you were dealing with such physical pain," Kim said, her eyes starting to well up. "I am so sorry. I will be praying that you get some real answers soon."

Once upon a time Lauren would have scoffed at the mention of prayer. But that was before she discovered a love relationship like no other she had ever known. A relationship so new that she was still completely overwhelmed with gratitude and joy.

"I can't tell you how much that means to me, Kim. Thank you."

"Now, I have a question for you. You don't have to say yes, but I would like you to consider something."

Lauren was intrigued. And a little nervous. "Okay."

"You see, all I've heard the last week is how amazing you are with Speckles, and how much he has changed because of your training. The general consensus among the team is that you should be Speckles' trainer."

Seeing Lauren's eyebrows go up, Kim quickly continued. "Speckles doesn't have a trainer because most people are scared of him. But he needs someone to work with him and exercise him. Someone he can learn to trust."

Lauren knew that Kim wanted the best for her horses as well as for the people working at Hope Reins. When the horses and volunteers were thriving, the kids who came benefited even more. It was one of the things Lauren admired about her.

"Lauren, let's face it. Speckles needs a safe person. That's what we want our trainers to be for our horses—a safe place. A person who learns to read them and understand them, and then lets the rest of us know what they need." Kim paused for a moment before adding, "So, what do you think?"

Lauren's mind raced. *Me, a trainer? For the most difficult horse at Hope Reins?* Yes, she had expressed interest, even shadowing a trainer during a few sessions. But she had assumed that her first horse would be one of the easygoing, laid-back ones. There was no way she was qualified for something like this. Still, Kim was waiting for an answer. She had to say something.

"Me?" was all she could get out.

"Yes, you. You are really good with him, and more important, he already trusts and respects you. I know you can do this. If it's not too much . . . I don't want you to do anything that will cause you more pain. Will you at least pray about it?"

Kim's eyes sparkled with hope. Lauren glanced at her daughters, their pleading stares willing her to answer. How could she possibly say no?

CHAPTER 7

SARAH STOPPED, closed her eyes, and let the sun warm her face before entering paddock two. Spring grass densely covered the field like a vibrant shag carpet, and the trees were already budding. *I can't believe it's been two months since I first met Joey.* Pulling back on the latch, she released the gate with a squeak. The Appaloosas turned toward the sound.

Sarah clutched a halter in both hands as she made her way to Joey. Kim had left a note for Sarah on the whiteboard in the hay shed asking if she would check on Joey after she finished feeding the herd.

Ever since Kim had discovered Sarah's past experience with an equine care and wellness team at a riding barn in Minnesota, she had been entrusting more and more of the horses' care to her. Sarah was happy to help and anxious for the chance to prove herself, especially after being at a loss for how to care for Joey that first morning.

The note also asked Sarah to check Joey's legs for any signs of rain rot—a bacterial skin infection common in light-colored horses, especially during wet months.

She gave Speckles a wide berth as she passed him. "I'm only here to check on Joey," she said. "You just do your thing, and I'll do mine."

Speckles flicked his ears at her, yawned, and then continued grazing.

Joey was resting near an oak tree. Sarah put the halter with an attached lead line over his head. "Hey, big guy." She ran her hand along his side. "You're looking good this morning."

The horse leaned his head into her shoulder in his usual trusting response.

Sarah clucked her tongue and began walking, and Joey followed on the lead line. And then, much to Sarah's surprise, so did Speckles, from fifteen feet away. As the brown-and-white horse approached, her shoulders tensed. She studied his awkward gait, his guarded eyes. He was the complete opposite of Joey.

Without thinking, Sarah dropped Joey's line and slowly approached Speckles. She stopped four feet in front of him, observing as he came closer. Then she cautiously extended her hand toward him. A moment later, his nose hit the target and Speckles sniffed her. When his lips parted, Sarah started to jerk her hand away, but the horse didn't strike or snap. So she relaxed her arm, keeping her hand under his muzzle. Soft, fleshy lips rooted around her hand, his whiskers tickling her.

"Maybe you aren't so scary after all," she whispered.

Just then Joey, who had quietly walked up behind Sarah, stomped his front hoof impatiently, startling her.

"Sheesh, Joey, way to interrupt a moment," she teased,

picking up his lead rope and navigating him to the gate. The two of them exited the field, leaving Speckles alone to graze.

Sarah led Joey over to a hitching post, one of the many wooden rails located throughout the Hope Reins property. As she stopped to secure Joey, he kept walking—right into the rail post. Joey came to an abrupt halt as his chest hit the barrier. *I hope no one saw that*, Sarah thought, quickly looking around. Thankfully, everyone was busy getting ready for a big group session with some kids from the Durham County foster care program.

In the short time Sarah had been volunteering at Hope Reins, she had learned a lot about sessions—the time when a child gets to work with a horse. She had even been asked to serve as a session leader. "You'd be a natural given your experience with horses," Kim had said, encouraging her to consider taking on the responsibility.

Sarah, however, was less confident. She loved working with animals, but she wasn't always as comfortable around people. Animals were easy to please. They loved you no matter what. The betrayal and hurt she had experienced growing up had taught her to keep a safe distance from people.

"Sorry about the post, Joey," Sarah said, wrapping the lead line around the rail. "I promise I really do have experience with horse care."

Joey shook off an annoying onslaught of flies.

"I just don't really have any experience with a blind horse," Sarah confessed.

Joey craned his head back, then bent down to nibble an itch on his upper front leg.

Sarah ran her hand along Joey's side and down each leg. All of his leg wounds were completely healed. Only a few scars remained where the deeper cuts had marred his skin. The large gash on his upper thigh had also healed, and hair was already growing back.

"You heal pretty quickly, Joey." Sarah made a second pass on each leg, looking for any scabs around the pasterns (ankles) or lower parts of the leg, telltale evidence of rain rot. All four legs looked good.

"I'll be right back, Joey," she said, giving his nose a good rub. Sarah made a dash for the nearby tack shed to grab some grooming supplies. When she emerged, Joey was nowhere to be seen! *How did he get loose? How could he have disappeared so quickly? And where did he go?* Her pulse quickened as she took in the empty arena.

The woods! "Please, Joey. Please don't be in the woods," she cried aloud. There were too many roots, holes, and low-hanging branches there, all potential hazards for a blind horse. Sarah raced to the edge of the woods, listening for any rustling sounds. Thankfully, there was no sign of the black-and-white beauty, just two squirrels romping through the fallen leaves. She glanced across the property to the parking lot. No horse on the run. She turned around, and there, as if following a trail of bread crumbs home, was Joey, sashaying back to his field without a care in the world. Sarah ran to catch up to him.

"Whoa there, big guy," she said, grabbing the lead rope that hung limply beside him. "Don't you *ever* wander off like that again," she said, surprised at how emotional she was getting.

Sarah let Joey graze for a few minutes while she calmed herself. "Okay, let's try this again," she said, turning Joey around and retracing their steps to the hitching post. She wound the rope tightly around the rail and started to clean dirt and leaves off Joey's back with a stiff bristle brush.

Just then, Sarah heard large vehicles pull into the gravel lot, followed by the sounds of excited children. Out of the corner of her eye, she saw a group of at least twenty kids being led by Kim across the ranch to the riding arena where Gabe and Shiloh waited.

I need to hurry. She wanted to finish Joey's grooming and get him back to his field before the kids left the demonstration and started to disperse around the ranch. As she picked up Joey's hoof to clean it out, Sarah noticed a boy fall back from the group, head over to Kim's office, and plop down in one of the rocking chairs on the little porch. Sarah expected someone from the foster care center to intervene, but everyone was at the arena.

What's he doing? Sarah wondered.

The boy appeared to be around twelve or thirteen, with messy, light brown hair. He wore baggy jeans and a faded Star Wars T-shirt.

Sarah watched the boy glance at his shoes and then toward the parking lot. *I need to do something.* After making sure Joey's rope was still secure, she commanded him to stay and walked over to the boy.

At that moment Sarah realized that knowing you *should* do something and knowing *what* to do are two very different things.

The boy's head was still turned toward the parking lot as Sarah approached.

"Hey," she said rather tentatively, "I noticed you sitting here all by yourself. Don't you want to see the horses?"

No answer. No eye contact. Nothing but silence.

"My name is Sarah. I volunteer here. What's your name?"

Silence.

"Do you . . . like horses?"

Deafening silence.

I am horrible at this. She glanced over at Joey, calmly standing at the hitching post.

"Ethan."

Okay. Progress.

"Hey, Ethan, nice to meet you. Whatcha doing over here?"

He didn't answer immediately. Then, "I had to come. They never give us a choice about anything. We're just here because all the girls begged to come. Horses are for girls."

"Well, you've got me there," Sarah confessed. "I'm a girl, and I do love horses, but I know lots of guys who like horses too."

She took a chance and sat down in the other rocking chair.

"What about all those tough cowboys in the Wild West?" she suggested. "They liked horses. And all the warriors on horseback in history that fought in battles. They probably really liked them."

He rolled his eyes. "Yeah, I guess."

Sarah cringed at the eye roll. "A lot of veterinarians are guys . . ." She stopped before she repeated herself once again.

You are trying way too hard to prove your point, she chided herself. Ethan picked at the rubber outsoles of his well-worn gray Converses. His fingernails, Sarah noticed, were in desperate need of a trim.

"We used to take my dog to the vet," Ethan said flatly. "He didn't like the guy too much."

"What kind of dog did you have?"

"I don't know, some kind of mutt. He was cool, though. His name was Bo."

"Bo is a cool name for a dog. I always wanted a dog when I was a kid, but my parents never let me. As soon as I can afford a house, I'm getting a dog."

Ethan stared at her, silent.

Sarah glanced at the group of children across the way. "You sure you don't want to head over there? I'll go with you."

"Nope, I'll just stay here till they drive us back." He looked at Sarah in defiance, adding, "You don't have to babysit me, you know."

I definitely prefer working with horses rather than people.

As if he heard her thoughts, Joey let out a loud nicker. He was digging the ground with his hoof, and Sarah knew she couldn't leave the horse alone any longer. But she didn't feel comfortable leaving Ethan alone either.

"Hey, would you like to meet a blind horse?"

"A blind horse?" he asked skeptically. "Doesn't he, like, fall down and stuff?"

"No, not at all. His name is Joey," she said, pointing toward the hitching post.

The boy stood up and started walking. Sarah had to run a few steps to catch up to him. He was taller than she had first thought, and he seemed to be all arms and legs, like a large-breed puppy who had yet to grow into his limbs.

Ethan came to an abrupt stop about ten feet in front of Joey and studied him. "He doesn't look blind."

"No, he doesn't," Sarah agreed. "You wouldn't know anything was wrong with him just by looking at him. After I finish grooming him, do you wanna help me get him back to his field?" she asked.

"I guess. What do you want me to do?"

"Well, first let me get some of this on him," she said, giving Joey a quick application of fly spray to help keep the pesky bugs away from his sensitive skin. "And this," she added, applying a dab of sunscreen on his pink freckled nose. "Now that the sun is getting more intense during the day, we don't want Joey to burn."

Sarah unwound Joey's lead rope and handed the end to Ethan. "Okay, follow me."

"Is he gonna bite me?" Ethan asked.

Sarah stroked Joey's neck. "No, Joey's really gentle, and I'll be right beside you."

Sarah caught Barb's attention as they walked by.

"Ethan, would you mind staying with Joey for a second while I ask my friend Barb a question?"

"Whatever," he mumbled.

"Hey, Barb," Sarah began, "is it okay if I take Ethan to paddock two? I promised he could help me with Joey."

"We saw the two of you talking," Barb said, smiling. "The counselors from the program were surprised you got him to say anything, let alone help with Joey."

"Why's that?"

"It turns out that Ethan has been a pretty tough nut to crack," Barb began. "According to his counselor, he is the oldest of four siblings who were placed into foster care after a teacher noticed the kids all showing up at school covered in bruises. Apparently, the foster family was terrific, but they only wanted to adopt the three younger kids."

"Ouch," Sarah winced, glancing back at Ethan, who was now totally preoccupied with Joey.

"Since then, they said, he's pretty much retreated inward," Barb continued. "Puts on a tough-as-nails facade and just keeps to himself."

Sarah couldn't imagine going through all of that at Ethan's age. Her childhood might not have been ideal either, but at least she had grown up with two parents who loved her. *Well, at least a mother who loved me*, she mentally clarified.

"If you've got him talking, that's a huge step forward," Barb continued, effectively bringing Sarah back to the present. "You two go ahead. I'll let the others know he's with you."

Slightly shaken from the painful memories she always tried so hard to keep hidden, Sarah plastered a smile on her face, nodded to Barb, and headed back to Ethan and Joey.

"Am I in trouble?" Ethan asked.

"What?" Sarah asked distractedly, before realizing the boy's concern. "Oh, no. Of course not. I was just letting Barb know that you are going to help me with Joey. It makes us look kind of bad when we lose a kid," she said, winking.

Ethan shrugged in reply.

When they came to the gate, Sarah released the latch, took the rope from Ethan, and led Joey into the field. Ethan stayed near the gate, outside the paddock. *How odd*, Sarah thought, seeing several of the wind chimes scattered on the ground. *That's the second time this week those have come down.*

Sarah unfastened Joey's halter. He gave his head a good shake, then called out to Speckles. A nicker came from the back of the field. While Joey decided whether to join his friend immediately, Sarah introduced Ethan to Joey.

"When he was younger, Joey was a champion, competing in different horse events—weren't you, boy?" She put her hand under Joey's chin, raising it to give him a kiss on the nose.

"But then he got hurt and couldn't compete anymore. His owners weren't able to keep him after that, and so he was sold. Actually, we think he was sold a bunch of times."

Joey nuzzled Sarah's shoulder. "Finally, Joey ended up with someone who couldn't—or actually wouldn't—take care of him."

"Why would you take a horse if you couldn't take care of it?" Ethan asked.

"I don't know," Sarah said, shaking her head. "But Joey's last owner pretty much just left him to die. This beautiful, sweet animal lying alone in his stall, thrown away and not wanted." Sarah's voice caught on the last two words. She hadn't really thought about the similarities in her story and Joey's. It caught her off guard. *Get it together, Sarah. This is about Joey and Ethan, not you.* Rubbing Joey's side, she swallowed hard against the pain and looked at Ethan.

He seemed ready to bolt again. He looked . . . angry. Or sad. Sarah couldn't tell.

"Do you want to greet Joey?"

He shrugged.

"Here, just hold your hand out like this." Sarah showed Ethan how to hold his hand palm down, fingers curved into an open fist. "Put it under Joey's nose so he can smell you. It's like a horse handshake."

Ethan put his hand over the fence. Immediately, Joey lowered his head and breathed onto the outstretched hand.

The transformation in Ethan's demeanor was instantaneous. "Cool. Can I touch him?"

"Sure," Sarah said, stepping aside.

"How did Joey end up here?" Ethan asked, gently rubbing Joey's back.

"Thankfully, a neighbor noticed something wasn't right and called the sheriff. Joey was rescued and taken to a foster family."

The boy's head jerked up.

"They have foster homes for horses?" he asked, his eyes widening.

"Huh, I hadn't thought about it like that before," Sarah said, chuckling. "But yes. Joey was in foster care until he came here."

"Is he happy here?" Ethan asked, eyes on Joey.

A breeze ruffled the boy's hair, lifting it off his forehead. He suddenly looked much younger to Sarah.

"I think he is," she answered. "I hope he is. Everyone here loves him. He seems to be adjusting well, and he's putting on weight. So, yes," she said, feeling more confident with her answer. "I think he is happy here."

Ethan watched Joey for a moment before saying, "I wonder if he misses his original family."

Sarah didn't know what to say. Could a horse miss someone? Did Joey remember what his life had been like before? She studied the boy as he studied Joey.

"Um—" Ethan motioned to the fence—"is it okay if I come in there?"

"Sure," Sarah said, opening the gate. *Wait! I should ask someone first,* she quickly thought. But everyone was far away. *We'll just stay close to the gate, and I'm sure it will be fine,* Sarah decided—hoping Barb would agree.

As Ethan entered the paddock, Sarah cast a quick glance at Speckles. His head was raised, assessing the new intruder, but he remained in the back of the paddock, making it clear he was not in the mood to be disturbed.

Ethan looked at Joey, then raised a questioning eyebrow to Sarah.

"Go ahead. Give him a good rub. He likes that," she encouraged, answering his unspoken question.

The boy's fingers splayed on Joey's back, the dirt under Ethan's fingernails matching the color of Joey's spots.

"Will he get to stay here forever?"

"Yes. This is his home now."

"That's good," he mumbled.

Squeals of delight drifted from the round pen where Gabe was engaging in some of his antics. The former party pony thrived on laughter. The louder his audience laughed, the more animated Gabe would become, pulling back his lips in an exaggerated smile and purposefully disregarding his trainer's commands. Sarah glanced at Ethan. The boy had lowered his head, and his shoulders were drooping. He looked defeated.

Joey craned his neck back, trying to sniff Ethan.

Ethan froze. "What's he doin'?"

"He just wants to say hi."

Ethan stepped in front of Joey and stretched an index finger toward Joey's head. His finger hovered over the horse's spotted forehead for several heartbeats before he gingerly touched the horse's face. One by one, each of the boy's fingers made contact until his entire hand lay flat against Joey's forehead.

"Are you sure he's really blind?"

"I'm sure."

Ethan stared into Joey's black eyes, then pulled his hand away and waved it in front of Joey.

"Can you see me?" he whispered.

Joey's sigh sent a stream of air rushing out of his nostrils.

Ethan stepped next to Joey and leaned his head on Joey's neck. Joey didn't move. Sarah stood transfixed by the boy and horse together. The image caused an unidentified longing to well up inside of her.

Joey flicked an ear in her direction, and then Sarah heard it—muffled crying.

Ethan's head was bowed, his hair hiding his eyes, his forehead pressed against Joey's neck.

Suddenly, Ethan's body tensed at the sound of children approaching. Sarah, not wanting to interrupt or embarrass Ethan, signaled to Barb that the group should move on. Barb took one look at Ethan, nodded, and moved the group to a different paddock. A few kids lingered behind the group, whining over missing the two "polka-dotted" horses. As Sarah stepped forward to ask Ethan if he would like to move farther back into the paddock, Joey turned his large head, effectively hiding the boy's face from view.

Sarah couldn't believe what she was seeing. *Joey is creating a shield around him.* The horse's strong, protective embrace broke through the last bit of control Ethan had. He threw his arms around Joey's neck and sobbed, his body shaking. Joey never moved. He stood fiercely and firmly, providing refuge for the weeping boy. Two deeply wounded creatures were giving and finding solace in one another. How much Sarah longed to join them.

Eventually Ethan's tears subsided, and he rubbed the sleeve of his shirt across his eyes. Sarah wanted to offer the boy a way to collect himself before heading back to the group. *Of course, the wind chimes!*

"Hey, Ethan," she called out, "before I get you back to the group, will you help me hang a few wind chimes back up?"

"Sure," he said, keeping his eyes averted.

"Thanks. It will only take a minute." She began collecting the chimes from the ground.

"Why are there so many wind chimes in here?"

Sarah recounted Joey's accident and explained how the wind chimes had helped him learn his boundaries so he didn't get injured like that again.

"I guess the feeders accidentally knocked these down when

they pushed the wheelbarrow in here this morning." She motioned to the top of a fence post. Ethan secured the chimes on the twine still hanging on the post and then ran his fingers through the chimes.

They hung two more chimes before heading back to the gate.

As they walked, Ethan kicked at rocks and chewed on his lower lip. Sarah could almost feel the tension begin to rise in him again.

"Are you okay?" Sarah asked, trying to sound nonchalant.

"I'm fine," he answered curtly. Sarah heard him take a deep breath. "Do you . . ." he started and then went silent again. "Do you . . . oh, never mind. It's stupid."

Sarah stopped at the gate. "Hey, look at me," she said gently. "Nothing you could say or ask me would be stupid. I'm not here to judge you. Trust me."

She could see the conflict in his eyes. He glanced at the large white cross on the other side of the ranch. Almost a full minute passed before he spoke.

"Do you believe in God?" he mumbled, his eyes immediately focusing on his shoes.

Wow. That was not what she was expecting. *Of all the questions he could have asked, of course it would be that one.* How was she supposed to answer his question? How did you explain to a wounded kid that you weren't sure what you believed anymore? That you'd been dealt a pretty bad hand in life and weren't really talking to God at the moment—that he had totally let you down?

It was pretty clear that Hope Reins was founded on Christian principles. Kim talked a lot about God and Jesus and hope. Sarah knew how she *should* answer. She knew how she would have answered once upon a time. But now? She chewed her lip as she considered Ethan's vulnerable question. *Say something*, Sarah commanded herself.

"You know what . . . I think I do." Hearing those words from her own lips emboldened her. She gave a decisive nod. "Yes," she clarified. "I do."

The two said good-bye to Joey and exited the field. Sarah didn't want the door of communication to shut completely yet, so she led Ethan to a nearby picnic table and motioned for him to sit next to her. To be perfectly honest, she was mad at God. For years, she had struggled with abandonment issues, betrayed by the two men in her life who should have stuck around. No, she didn't actually doubt there was a God. She just wasn't sure he cared about her that much.

Now it was her turn to ask the question. "Do *you* believe in God?"

"I don't know," Ethan admitted. "I think I used to when I was little. My real parents . . . they took us to church a few times, and I kind of liked it. They had snacks and games and stuff. But now, I'm just not sure. I guess maybe God's real, but not the way I used to think he was."

"In what way do you think he's different now than when you were little?"

Ethan picked up a piece of hay off the bench and tied it in a knot. "I used to think God was nice and that he wanted to help us and stuff, but . . ."

He didn't finish. He didn't have to. How many times had she asked God why he hadn't prevented her father's accident? Or his betrayal? How many times had she begged God to save her marriage? Her stomach cramped up with a wave of fresh pain—and fear. What if Kim and the others found out about her past, about the things she had done to try to numb the pain, and hurt those who had hurt her? What if they discovered her lack of faith? Her pretense? Would they condemn her? Want her to leave? She couldn't imagine having to leave this place. *I can never let them know about my past. I need to keep it together and convincingly play the role of the good Christian with a strong faith.*

Yet, suddenly she wished that she *did* have a strong faith, so she could offer the boy some thread of hope.

"Honestly, Ethan, I don't know why God allows certain things to happen. In fact, I've asked those same questions many, many times." Unsure of what to say next, Sarah found herself silently praying for the first time in years. *God, this boy needs you. I know I haven't talked to you in a long time, and I'm sorry about that, but would you . . .* She paused, glancing at Ethan. His shoulders were bent, his head low. *God, will you please help me know what to say? Help me help him somehow. Amen.*

And then she waited for an answer, a sign . . . something.

A hawk soared high above the trees. Squirrels chattered along a branch. A horse neighed from the far pasture. But no words were spoken from above. Sarah suddenly felt foolish.

"Thanks."

"Thanks? For what?" Sarah asked, bewildered.

"For being honest," he said. "Most adults just tell kids what they think we need to hear. I like that you were honest and said you don't know."

Sarah was dumbfounded.

As they walked back toward the Hope Reins office where they had met an hour ago, Ethan shoved his hands in his jean pockets. "I hope I can come back here sometime."

"What!" Sarah answered in an overly dramatic voice. "Come back to the horse place? I thought horses were just for girls."

Her words were met with a lopsided grin. "Well, most of them are." He shrugged. "But Joey . . . he's pretty cool."

Just then, Kim rang a loud cowbell, signaling it was time for the group to gather around the fire pit for closing time activities. Sarah pointed and whispered, "Go join the others."

To her utter surprise, the boy complied.

Something powerful had just happened. Was it possible that God had used a blind horse to touch a hurting boy's heart? Did God care about such things? *Maybe he hasn't forgotten about me after all?*

Sarah turned back, looking at the fields where horses grazed. *I love this place.* The peace. The hope. The . . . healing. Each one waiting to be found.

CHAPTER 8

FOUR WEEKS AFTER her coffee date with Kim, Lauren sat on a mounting block inside the training arena, her head in her hands, silent sobs shaking her sore body. A frustrated Speckles stood on the opposite side, snorting and pawing at the dirt.

She had been trying to get him to lunge, a basic training component where the horse walks or trots around the trainer in a circle while on a long lead line—a necessary skill so that the horse can get exercise without exhausting its trainer. She'd seen other trainers do it at Hope Reins dozens of times. She'd even lunged several of the other horses there. Yet whenever she asked Speckles to move, he reared up and kicked his back legs out at her.

They had been at it for weeks, and she was no closer to getting him to lunge than when they started. In fact, he seemed to be getting worse. The harder she pushed, the more fiercely he pushed back.

Maybe he's simply untrainable. Or maybe he just doesn't have the right trainer.

As Lauren massaged her temples in an attempt to fend off the tension headache she could feel coming on, a large brown chin bumped her elbow. Lauren's entire body tensed. And then, with a long chuffing declaration, a chin was gently lowered onto her lap.

Speckles stood with his head in Lauren's lap for several seconds before he shifted his weight and pulled his back leg gingerly off the ground. As he moved his leg, Lauren heard a distinct clicking sound. The sound—like that of a loud knuckle crack—sent shivers down her spine.

Lauren carefully lowered her hands from her head so that she could see the horse. She didn't move or talk—just observed. Speckles continued to shift his weight, each time lifting one of his back legs off the ground about five or six inches, his head never leaving her lap.

After a few minutes, Lauren's knee began to throb, and as much as she hated to make Speckles move, she had to extend her leg. Otherwise, her knee would lock, and . . .

"Oh, my poor boy," she gasped, looking into Speckles' eyes. "Your legs hurt, don't they?"

She reached out hesitantly, barely touching the brown muzzle that looked as if it had been splashed with white paint in the middle.

"You're in pain, aren't you, boy?"

Lauren studied Speckles as if seeing him for the first time. He shifted again, and again she heard a click. His front legs appeared tense, muscles twitching. His lips were held together in a tight line.

How had she not noticed it until now? The kicking, the bucking—throwing Barb's daughter off. If Speckles was in such excruciating pain, of course he wouldn't want to carry any weight, especially a rider. Of course he would want to avoid a woman who came in every day and wanted him to keep moving. *You weren't untrainable; you were suffering.*

It all made perfect sense now. Lauren had heard that Speckles had never been allowed to run or exercise at the stud farm. When the Equine Rescue League found him, his feet were in atrocious condition. Lauren might not have had a ton of experience with horses, but she did have a master's degree in immunology and advanced training in biotechnology. Was it possible that Speckles was showing symptoms of degenerative joint disease? She racked her brain, trying to remember some of her previous training from what seemed like a lifetime ago. Couldn't such a joint disease be brought on by a septic infection—like one that could happen from standing, immobile, knee deep in one's own filth and muck for so long?

Lauren moaned, frustrated that she hadn't put this together before. Yes, she had been busy trying to learn all she could about horse training—shadowing other trainers, reading books, and even attending an equestrian training seminar in Rocky Mount.

She had been so busy learning how to train *a* horse that she had neglected to study *her* horse. Lauren slowly stood up to bend and flex her knee. The pain had become excruciating. Again, she wondered how she had not seen it before. How many times had she lashed out at others because of her unrelenting pain? And when she couldn't lash out, she retreated, as if she could somehow hide from the pain.

"You big ol' speckled monster," Lauren said, a sudden protectiveness welling up inside of her. "You aren't a bad horse. You're just hurting." She stroked his white speckled back. "I'm so sorry I missed that. Forgive me?"

The horse exhaled, making a gentle whooshing sound.

"Don't you worry," she said, placing one hand on either side of his face, like a parent consoling a frightened child. "We'll figure this out. I promise." She walked to the gate where she had thrown his lead line earlier, after he had reared up and kicked at her. When she turned back to the horse, she was surprised to find him walking toward her. Her throat tightened with emotion.

"I know, boy," she said, closing the distance between them and running her hand along his neck.

"Trust me. I know."

Later that afternoon, Lauren shared her suspicions with Kim. The founder of Hope Reins couldn't believe that she hadn't put two and two together herself. The next day, Kim called Dr. Gallagher, who asked to see Speckles at the equine center at the university. Lauren, grateful that her own knee was feeling better, accompanied Kim and Speckles to the appointment. Not surprisingly, he wasn't at all pleased to be put on a trailer. But the reward of a full bag of carrots was enticing, and Kim and Lauren managed to get Speckles in and out of the trailer. At the equine center, the women watched as Dr. Gallagher and his interns put Speckles through a battery of tests. By the looks on their faces, Lauren knew the diagnosis was not going to be good.

"Well, we've got some answers for you," Dr. Gallagher said, looking up from Speckles' last X-ray. "Speckles has some pretty advanced arthritis and a locking stifle." Responding to Lauren's puzzled look, he explained. "His knees are getting stuck in an upward position, causing him to try to kick them back into place."

"So he isn't necessarily kicking at us, but kicking against the pain?" Lauren asked hopefully.

Dr. Gallagher momentarily pondered the question. "You know, I imagine it might be a little bit of both," he said with a wink.

"We've got to remember," Dr. Gallagher said, "that Speckles came from a bad situation where he probably learned some bad habits. Add to that intense pain and fear, and you've got yourself a very difficult horse to work with."

The procedure room they were standing in suddenly felt cold. *A very difficult horse.* The words played through Lauren's mind like a taunting echo. And yet, his diagnoses only confirmed the bond Lauren felt to the horse.

Dr. Gallagher led them to the small enclosure where Speckles was being kept. The horse seemed oddly mellow.

"We've got him on some pretty strong pain meds right now, so he should be just fine for the ride back. And I'm sending you home with two different medications. One is an anti-inflammatory, which he will take every day for several weeks, at which point I'll come out and reevaluate him. The other is a painkiller to be used as needed."

Why does having a plan always help things seem better? Lauren marveled, feeling encouraged for the first time all day.

"Oh, and given how bad his knees are, no riding. Light exercise should help the locking stifle, but the combination of the stifle and the arthritis will make riding incredibly painful for him."

Lauren glanced at Kim. No riding? Although riding was not the focus of Hope Reins, the ranch was dedicated to helping kids by allowing them to build a relationship with a horse. Riding was one aspect of that relationship. What would these new restrictions mean for Speckles? Would he still have a home at Hope Reins?

I sure hope so, Lauren thought. Because she was committed to doing everything in her power to help the speckled horse.

"Of course we are going to keep him," Kim assured Lauren on the way home. "It's not his fault that he's in such bad shape. But we do need to figure out how to help him, how to work with him, and in what capacity he might be able to work with children—if at all," she added.

Lauren took Kim's words to heart as a challenge. For the next two weeks, she visited the library, watched countless YouTube videos, and pored over multiple online articles to formulate a plan. A plan was a good first step. The harder part would be getting over her fears. She had been so shaken by her last training session, when his hooves missed her face by mere inches. And then, hearing Dr. Gallagher describe Speckles' condition, Lauren was afraid of accidentally hurting him during training. She desperately wanted to help the horse. But how?

The answer came in one of the instructional videos on lunging horses. The training used the elements of natural horsemanship. Lauren had never heard of that approach before, but it made perfect sense. Instead of using pain or force, it paired a horse's natural instincts and methods of communication with the application and release of pressure, provided by her body and a lightweight fiberglass training stick. The idea was to provide a gentler approach to training, slowly infringing upon the horse's personal space and then retreating, gradually increasing his tolerance. It seemed like it might be the best fit for Speckles. Lauren gathered as much information on the technique as possible.

But before she subjected Speckles to the new training, she decided to implement natural horsemanship techniques on her two Welsh corgi dogs, much to the surprise of her husband, Rick.

"What in heaven's name are you doing?" he asked her one afternoon as she stood in their backyard holding a leash— actually three leashes tied together—in her hand, while one of her dogs, Dunie, ran around her in big circles.

Lauren smiled sheepishly. "Can't you tell? I'm lunging the dog. Gotta be ready for Speckles tomorrow, you know."

Rick knew all too well how his wife of fifteen years poured herself into a project. He simply shook his head, deposited the bag of trash he was carrying into the container, and returned to the house. Lauren slowed Dunie down to a walk. Her dogs had done a great job lunging, but they were nothing like Speckles. Would it really be any different? Would a slower pace and the use of pressure and release really make any difference in the difficult horse?

Only time would tell.

———— · ————

The next day, Lauren arrived at Hope Reins late in the afternoon to begin Speckles' new, slower-paced training. After retrieving a rope-style halter and lead, a long lunge line, and a training stick, she led Speckles to the round arena. A new training style required a new training atmosphere. The horse walked compliantly beside her. However, Joey did not seem too happy about the absence of his pasture-mate, crying and whinnying while he paced the fence line. The sounds nearly broke Lauren's heart.

"I'm just borrowing him for a little while, Joe-Joe. I promise to bring him right back."

The two Appaloosas had formed quite a bond over the past few weeks. Ever since Speckles had stopped bullying Joey at feeding time, the two had become inseparable. They grazed together, ran together, and nuzzled together. Anytime Joey lost track of Speckles, they began their own version of Marco Polo, neighing to each other until they were reunited. Lauren had even witnessed Speckles leading Joey around the paddock by nibbling at his rump, effectively directing the blind horse where he wanted him to go. In fact, in many ways Speckles seemed to have become Joey's eyes. Lauren wondered if Joey really even needed the wind chimes anymore. He had definitely learned where the fencing and trees were.

Joey's cries intensified as Lauren led Speckles into the round pen. Once she stopped, Speckles let loose an earsplitting whinny. Lauren rubbed her ears.

"What in the world was that?"

He bobbed his head as a quiet answering neigh came from paddock two. And then . . . silence. Lauren peered through the gate toward Joey, who was now standing in the corner of the paddock, as close as he could get to the round pen.

"Are you telling your friend where you are?" Lauren asked, amazed at the way the two horses had learned to communicate with one another. "You two are unbelievable, you know that? Okay," she said, taking a step back, "let's show your friend what you can do."

Lauren was determined to spend the first few minutes of their session simply observing Speckles. If she detected he was in pain, she would ask nothing from him. First, she had him take a few steps forward. His legs seemed more relaxed today. His lips were loose and pliable, and his ears were forward and up. Hopefully, the medications were giving him some relief.

Lauren attached the lunge line and tapped gently on his shoulder with the training stick. She was still getting used to switching to the stick rather than flinging the attached rope at his feet to get him to move. That method was effective for some of the other horses, but obviously not for Speckles.

"Let's just try a slow walk, okay, big boy?"

She steadied herself for a possible bad reaction. Speckles started walking. It was a slow and cautious walk, but it was a walk. Not wanting to push her luck, she stopped after two rotations. It didn't seem like rocket science. She just used the training stick in a different way inviting him to walk rather than trying to force him.

"You did it, buddy! Good job!" Lauren fed him a carrot she had hidden in her pocket.

Speckles eagerly accepted the treat. Lauren unclipped his line in order to let him explore for a little while. *I can't push him too hard.* As she walked toward the gate, she was startled to discover that Speckles was following her. Wanting to see if it was purposeful or not, she changed directions and walked toward the back of the arena. Within minutes, a slobbery chin was tapping her shoulder. Without thinking, she reached up and hugged the horse.

Startled, Speckles jerked his head back.

"Oh, bud, I'm sorry. I wasn't thinking." Too much affection too soon.

Yet she was grateful to see a more playful and trusting side of him. She walked across the arena again. It took Speckles a few minutes, but he eventually followed. This time, she slowly reached out a hand and stroked his neck. Speckles turned his large head toward her in an awkward horse hug.

"I love you, you difficult, sweet bully," Lauren said.

Lauren returned Speckles to the paddock where Joey waited anxiously. The two nuzzled each other as if they had been separated for years instead of mere minutes. Joey began nibbling Speckles' back up and down as if he were giving him a rubdown following a strenuous workout. Lauren laughed out loud.

The difference in Speckles' behavior was remarkable. Now that he was feeling better, he had become a much more cordial companion for Joey. In fact, if Lauren didn't know better, she'd have sworn Speckles was starting to take care of Joey.

"You know, Speckles, you might not be able to be ridden," she said aloud, "but it's pretty clear that you have a purpose out here—just as much as each one of the other horses does."

As if understanding exactly what the human in his field had just said, Speckles nickered. Lauren laughed at his response.

"In fact, maybe you have more than one purpose."

She blew the horse a good-night kiss.

CHAPTER 9

By LATE SPRING, the sessions were in full swing. The warm temperatures, the longer days, and the lighter school day schedules made it easier to offer late afternoon or early evening sessions. That flexibility also worked well for Sarah.

The day after the big event at Hope Reins with the foster kids, Sarah had gone by the office. She had forgotten to take her volunteer's T-shirt the day before. Expecting an empty office, Sarah was startled to find Kim sitting inside. "Oh, sorry to interrupt," Sarah said, about to turn around.

"No, please, come in and sit for a few minutes," Kim said. The previous day had been nonstop and Kim had barely been able to catch her breath, let alone debrief with Sarah. But she certainly had heard about the interaction between her volunteer and Ethan.

"You are a natural, Sarah. I don't know how you broke through his barrier, but everyone was impressed—including me."

Sarah was a little uncomfortable with the unsolicited praise, and yet it made her hungry for more. "He's a great kid and just needed somebody to listen to him."

Kim looked intently at Sarah. "Would you consider becoming a session leader? Or at least come out and shadow a session? We desperately need more session leaders, and it's like God just brought you to us when we needed you the most."

Sarah's stomach lurched. *Ugh, why did she have to bring God into this? How would Kim feel if she knew the truth—knew who I really was? Would she take back her offer?*

"Well?" Kim asked, her eyes sparkling with anticipation. "What do you think?"

Whether it was Kim's kind nature, her pleading eyes, or her own vulnerability, Sarah didn't know. But whatever the reason, she had said yes.

She had been shadowing Barb for five sessions now. Although Barb kept insisting to Sarah that she was ready to lead a session on her own, her "student" made it clear she was just fine to keep things as they were. And then Barb got sick.

The two of them were doing cleanup chores around the ranch when Barb started coughing. "Hey, Sarah . . ." She cleared her throat and started again. "I thought I could make it through the entire day, but this cold is getting worse. Would you mind covering my session for me? The little girl's file is on the table in the office. She'll be here at 6:00."

"Of course. I'd be happy to," Sarah replied, feigning confidence. "You go home and get some rest."

Mouthing a grateful thank-you, Barb headed for her car. Sarah quickly checked the time on her phone. *She'll be here in twenty minutes.* Sarah glanced around the feed shed. She loved the cozy little room and was tempted not to leave. *Just shut the door and hide out until everyone is gone.*

No, take a deep breath. You can do this. Sarah closed the shed door, secured the padlock, and headed to the office. The file was sitting on the table right where Barb said it would be.

She pulled out the referral sheet and scanned the information.

Child: Aly, age five.
Living situation: Adopted from foster care when she
    was two years old by Cindy, a single mom who lives
    in Durham.
Caregiver remarks: Aly is very shy and withdrawn. Doesn't
    talk much. Won't engage with other children. Very
    inward and hesitant in new situations.

There were some similarities with Ethan—"withdrawn," "doesn't talk much," "won't engage with other children"—but until she met this little girl, Sarah wasn't sure what to do. *How would Barb help the little girl feel at ease?* Her thoughts were interrupted by a car door slamming, followed by another. *That must be them.* She slipped the referral sheet back in the folder, wiped her hands on the front of her jeans, and went out to meet them.

Shading her eyes from the sun, Sarah was able to make out a thin, athletic-looking woman leading a petite little girl toward the Hope Reins office. The girl looked fragile, as if the slightest gust of wind could knock her over. Her thick brown curls were pulled into a ponytail that bounced when she walked. Her eyes were fixed on the stuffed bunny she was clutching.

"Hi," Sarah said, waving. "Are you Cindy and Aly?"

The woman nodded. "That's us."

"It's so nice to meet you both," Sarah said, extending her hand first to Cindy and then to Aly.

The girl's knuckles whitened as she dug her fingers into the bunny.

"I like your bunny," Sarah said, pretending to shake the bunny's hand. "I'm Sarah, and I get to hang out with you today."

Deep brown eyes momentarily glanced up at her—eyes full of fear and distrust. Aly's bottom lip turned in slightly, evidence that she was chewing the inside of her cheek.

"Aly and I are happy to meet you, Sarah. Aren't we, Aly?" Cindy nodded, as if willing her daughter to mimic the movement. She did not.

Sarah wondered how she was going to connect with the stoic girl. "Well, Aly," she said, "the first thing you get to do is pick out a horse that you would like to spend some special time with. Would you like to go meet my horse friends?"

Aly's slight nod indicated she had heard Sarah's question, but she didn't move.

"Sweetie, why don't you let me hold Mr. Bunny? We don't want the horses to think he's a toy and try to eat him," Cindy said softly. Aly's eyes briefly filled with horror, and she quickly passed the sand-colored bunny to her mother.

"Have fun, sweetie," Cindy whispered to Aly. "Listen to Miss Sarah and tell those horses hi for me, okay?"

Aly's eyes never left the ground. *And then there were two,* Sarah thought, as Cindy made her way to the picnic tables, where PJ began talking with her. Hope Reins had special volunteers trained to be a listening ear for the caregivers of the children in sessions.

"Okay, Miss Aly. Are you ready to go find a horse?"

Sarah smiled when the girl nodded again. Sarah started

walking, expecting Aly to follow, but she didn't. On a whim, Sarah held out her hand toward the child and was surprised when a tiny hand touched her palm. Closing her fingers around Aly's cold hand, she led her toward the paddock where Shiloh was standing near the fence.

"This is Shiloh," Sarah said, crouching down to Aly's eye level. The girl smelled like peanut butter. "She's a sweet pony who was given to us by a nice family who couldn't keep her anymore. She loves rainstorms and playing in mud puddles."

Aly just stared at the ground. Sarah tried again.

"Shiloh was moved to this paddock because it doesn't have any grass, just dirt. She was eating too much grass and getting bad stomachaches. We feed her hay instead. But I think she's happy."

Nothing. *Okay*, she thought, changing tactics.

"And that," she said, pointing to the brownish-black mare in the middle of the field, "is Cadence. We don't know much about where she came from. We got her from a group that rescues horses that are being treated badly."

No reaction.

Shiloh reached under the fence to get to a particularly tempting clump of grass in front of Aly.

Aly took a step back to put more distance between her and the horse.

Sarah kept talking. "Shiloh and Cadence are good friends because they both get a little nervous and shy around new people and new things. They help each other feel brave."

Aly did not seem impressed or interested in either horse.

Okay, strike one.

Still clasping Aly's hand, Sarah moved to the paddock that Essie, a donated chestnut Morgan horse with a white strip down her muzzle, now shared with Jesse, a rescued mare. The small bay-colored quarter horse had come to the ranch broken and in need of gentle care and understanding. The poor creature had been saved from horrific conditions by the equine rescue league. When they found her, she was 150 pounds underweight, mysteriously missing half her tongue, and terrified of people. Desperate to give Jesse the opportunity to trust again, Kim and Barb had visited her several times at the foster ranch.

Eventually Jesse softened toward them and began to show a strength of will and determination that had deeply moved both women. Jesse was still a work in progress, but she had found a home at Hope Reins, and, given time, Kim believed she would become a favorite among the children.

Sarah introduced the two mares to Aly, giving her a little bit of their backstory. Aly seemed mesmerized by Jesse, but when Sarah asked her if she wanted to spend time with these two horses, there was no response.

Strike two.

On to paddock two.

"And these boys are Joey and Speckles," Sarah said. "Joey is the one by the hay box, and Speckles is way over there in the back of the field."

Joey lifted his head at the sound of visitors. "Joey is blind, so he can't see you, but he can definitely hear us. He knows we're here." Aly's eyes grew wide.

Joey began to saunter in their direction, stopping near the fence.

"Hi, Joey," Sarah said, extending her hand. "This is my friend Aly."

The little girl raised her head and tilted it almost all the way back to take in the large horse standing before her. *He must look like a giant to her. He certainly makes her look tiny.*

Aly couldn't take her eyes off the horse.

Joey's nostrils widened and twitched, and he lowered his head in search of something. He sniffed at the ground, extended his head under the fence, then pulled it back again. He repeated this several times before finally zeroing in on what he was hunting for—Aly.

His nose bumped her leg.

The girl didn't move.

Joey's lips became animated in his classic "there's a treat hiding somewhere, and I'm gonna find it" way.

The peanut butter! Sarah had smelled it on Aly, so Joey certainly would too. Not wanting Joey to frighten the little girl, Sarah retrieved a treat from her pocket, clucked her tongue to get Joey's attention, and then handed it to him.

"Joey and his friend Speckles came to Hope Reins a few months ago," Sarah explained, watching Aly observe Joey's every move.

Joey made quick work of the treat, then stuck his head back through the fence in search of the delicious-smelling girl. Aly's shoulders flinched, but then she leaned forward ever so slightly, oblivious to everything except Joey. Sarah couldn't believe it.

"Joey used to be a champion jumper," Sarah said, sitting down on the grass beside the young girl. "He won lots of pretty ribbons, but then he got hurt and couldn't jump anymore."

Aly sat down beside her and looked at Sarah—in the eye. Sarah was caught off guard for a moment.

"Joey's owners couldn't keep him anymore, so he was sold a couple of times. The last owner didn't take very good care of him, and Joey almost died. But Ms. Kim, the woman who started this ranch, believes that God has a plan for Joey's life, and so she brought him here to live."

Aly had been staring at Sarah the entire time she was relating Joey's story. Sarah could hear children laughing across the ranch, obviously enjoying their sessions with the horses. Would Aly ever get to that point? The volunteer and the little girl sat quietly by the fence. When Aly raised her eyebrows with an unspoken question, Sarah answered instinctively with her own question.

"Aly, do you want to touch Joey?"

Aly nodded. The two of them stood up, and once again, Sarah clucked her tongue to get Joey's attention.

"Joey, put your head up here so Aly can say hi."

Joey responded as if he had known that command his entire life, stepping closer to the fence and holding his head still. Sarah directed Aly's hand to Joey's shoulder, showing her how to gently pet him. Aly followed her instructions perfectly, and Sarah rewarded Joey with another treat.

"Great job, Aly. Joey really likes you," she said, encouragingly. Sarah paused, then added, "Would you like to go meet some other horses?"

Aly shook her head. A slight shake, but an unmistakable one. She had found her horse.

Sarah smiled. "Well, then, would you like to learn how to brush him?"

Aly's bobbing ponytail spoke volumes. Sarah led the girl to the tack shed, where they collected supplies—a halter and lead line, a grooming bucket full of brushes, and a hoof pick. Then they walked back to Joey's paddock.

"You stay on the outside of the fence, Aly, and I'll go get Joey."

As Sarah went through the open gate, her boot got tangled

up in something. *One of Joey's wind chimes.* "How did this get here?" she mumbled, grabbing the object and tossing it over the fence. *I'll get to you later.* Sarah could see that Aly was watching closely as she put the halter on Joey. Once they were outside the paddock, Sarah let Aly help her hold Joey's lead line.

In the grooming area, Sarah took out two brushes and handed the rubber currycomb to Aly. "First we use this round brush to get the dirt off Joey's coat. Brushing the horses is one way we take care of them. They get lots of dirt and leaves and even bugs in their coats, and they need us to help get those things off."

The little girl nodded as Sarah showed Aly how to brush in small circles.

"You know, all of our horses need lots of love and care," Sarah said, feeling the need to fill the silence. "But since Joey can't see, he needs even more love and care." She moved Aly's hand down a little lower on Joey's side. "There you go. I see lots of dirt on his coat right there. Good job, Aly."

The little girl acknowledged the compliment with a shy glance as she continued brushing.

"Now let's switch brushes." Sarah gave Aly the hard-bristled brush. "We brush in short, straight strokes with this one, to remove everything the currycomb loosened." Sarah demonstrated the technique along Joey's back. And then she stopped. *Wait. Aly will never be able to reach this high.*

"I have an idea. Let's move Joey closer to this picnic table." Sarah loosened Joey's lead rope a little and maneuvered him a few steps.

"Okay, Aly, if you stand on top of the picnic table, you can brush Joey's back. I'll be right here beside you."

Aly concentrated on her job, and Joey's coat started to gleam.

Sarah finished the overall grooming with a soft brush and then gave Joey a light hoof cleaning.

"All done. Thank you, Aly. You were a great help. Would you like to walk Joey with me?"

Aly nodded, yet there was a look—a longing—in her expression.

"Were you hoping to *ride* Joey today?"

Another nod. Wow! The timid little girl wanted to ride the large blind horse. Well, what girl doesn't want to ride a horse! Aly was young enough to not give a second thought to Joey's condition, something none of the adults at Hope Reins seemed able to do. It suddenly dawned on Sarah that no one had ridden Joey since he arrived at Hope Reins—since the incident with the fence.

It seemed that no one wanted to risk Joey getting hurt again, so they just let him be. Sarah didn't even know if Joey had a specific trainer. Surely someone worked with him, or else they wouldn't be able to use him in sessions, but was anyone getting him ready to carry a rider? Looking at the hopeful little face staring up at her, Sarah knew she would have to ask.

"Hey, Aly," she said, bending down to be eye to eye with the girl. "Can I tell you a little secret?"

Deep brown eyes blinked at her, looking quite serious.

Sarah lowered her voice to a whisper. "This is my first time doing a session all by myself, and I don't know if Joey can take kids for a ride yet," she confessed. "Joey hasn't been here that long, and I think he's still getting used to his new home, all the new people, and the other horses."

Aly looked at Joey, then back at Sarah.

"But you know what? Maybe you can help Joey start to feel

more comfortable here so that one day soon he might be able to give rides."

Aly tilted her head just the way Joey often did.

Sarah smiled at the similarity.

"Yeah," she said, warming to her own idea. "Maybe each time you come to Hope Reins, you can groom Joey and talk to him and just be his friend—to help him build trust in people. Do you think you could do that for Joey?"

Aly nodded—a firm, decisive nod. Sarah had no doubt whatsoever that Aly would keep her end of the deal. The new partners walked Joey around the large riding arena twice before leading him back to his paddock.

Sarah stopped Joey in front of the gate.

"Since you are going to be one of Joey's best friends, I bet he would like to give you a hug. Is that okay?"

Aly's ponytail bobbed quickly up and down.

Sarah positioned Aly at Joey's left shoulder. Then Sarah reached into her pocket and pulled out an apple-and-oat biscuit. She held it in front of Joey's nose, and the horse followed her hand as she moved it toward his left shoulder.

As Joey took the treat from Sarah's hand, he effectively covered Aly in an equine embrace, much like the one he had given Ethan. Joey lingered for a moment with his head wrapped around little Aly. Suddenly, he surprised both of them by sticking out his tongue and rolling it across Aly's cheek.

Aly's head jerked back. Her eyes widened with shock. But her face lit up with a genuine smile, revealing an adorable dimple on her left cheek. *Joey, you're such a charmer.*

Sarah laughed out loud. "Joey just gave you a kiss! He must really, really like you."

Aly's eyes twinkled with delight as Sarah secured the

gate. Joey's job was done for the night as he made a beeline for Speckles. The two nuzzled and nibbled each other before Speckles began walking toward the back pasture with Joey following close behind.

Sarah and Aly walked hand in hand back to the Hope Reins office, where Cindy was waiting.

"Well, sweetie, how did it go?" she said, holding Aly's hands.

Sarah couldn't see Aly's face, but she definitely could see Cindy's face as her daughter threw her arms around her mom and squeezed tight. There was so much love expressed by the young mother, hope glistening in her tear-filled eyes. Sarah found her own eyes starting to well up.

Maybe God really does have a purpose for Joey. And if so, maybe someday he might even have some kind of plan for me.

Sarah walked Cindy and Aly to their car, then returned to the office to jot down a few notes about the session:

Aly made a strong connection to Joey. Wants to build trust with him. Interested in riding at some point, if possible. Likes horse hugs. Didn't speak once during session.

Sarah wasn't sure if Barb would take over Aly's sessions when the little girl came back, but she found herself hoping that wouldn't be the case. Maybe she would ask Kim about being Aly's session leader going forward. *Just for the sake of continuity,* Sarah thought as she walked to her car. But she knew full well that her desire to work with Aly went much deeper than that.

CHAPTER 10

"BARB, HOW ARE WE supposed to pay this?" Kim asked, holding the vet bill in her hand. "We don't have the money."

The women stared at the bill—$1,700 for Essie's latest visit to the animal hospital for another bout of severe colic. The tests and treatments had quickly added up.

"We've been tight for months, but between a pretty steady stream of donations and a relatively healthy herd, we were doing okay. But now . . ." Kim's voice trailed off as she stared at the stack of bills in front of her. Along with the vet bill, there was another thousand due for hay, five hundred for supplements and grain, eight hundred owed to the farrier, three hundred for repairs made on the tractor, and . . . . Kim couldn't bring herself to look at the insurance bill.

She looked at Barb. Steady, rock-solid, faith-filled Barb.

"I know it looks bad, Kim," Barb said. "But God will provide. Somehow, someway, he will provide."

How does she keep such faith?

"But, Barb, there is nothing there," Kim said.

Barb looked at the bills. "What I do know is the God we trust is the same God who fed five thousand people from one little boy's lunch, and who rained manna down from heaven to feed an entire nation. He can do this, Kim."

She spoke with such confidence that Kim couldn't help but feel a little more hopeful. But still, she was the leader of this ranch. Surely she should know what to do, know how to make ends meet. Had starting this ministry been a terrible mistake?

Self-doubt began to fill Kim's mind. Because God had provided the land in such a miraculous way, she had just assumed he would throw open every door, take care of every obstacle they encountered in a similar way. He provided, yes. But nothing like with the land. Everything else had come slowly, painfully.

Money had been the hardest of all. For someone who took great comfort in financial security, who delighted in having a healthy savings account, the ranch finances had been a nightmare. Determined not to dip into her family's personal savings account, Kim had purchased most everything needed for the ranch on credit—credit that was maxed out. Donations had been trickling in, but there just never seemed to be enough. Never enough to make her feel like she could breathe easily or that they could plan for the ministry's future. Every day was an act of faith. *And I don't think my faith is strong enough to get us through,* she thought.

At first, when excitement ran high, it had been so easy to have faith. But when the horses needed hay in the bitter cold of January and the scorching heat of July and the upkeep of the ranch seemed never-ending, the mounting bills punctured the elation. Kim couldn't keep the accusing thoughts at bay.

Some kind of leader you are; you're going to fail and let them all down. They pummeled her until she was paralyzed with fear. Mike tried to reassure and comfort her, but in many ways Kim wanted to prove herself to him most of all. *If only I had faith like Barb's.*

Worry and trust.

"I need some air," Kim said suddenly.

Barb nodded in understanding. Kim knew that Barb would begin praying for her as soon as she left, and that brought her momentary comfort.

The sun's warmth felt good. She breathed deeply, taking in the wonderful fragrances of June flowers in bloom. A volunteer had asked if she could plant flowers on the property, and what a colorful masterpiece she had created. Gardenias, hydrangeas, roses, and marigolds dotted the landscape, and flowering vines and shrubs emitted intoxicating aromas.

So much beauty. And yet so much stress. Mike and Barb provided constant encouragement, and the Hope Reins board of directors were working on possible solutions to the cash flow problem. But this had all been her idea. Her calling. Her dream. Her burden to carry. Her problem to solve.

Kim walked down the long fence line, greeting each horse she passed. A few raised their heads in response, a couple rested contentedly, and several were too far away to hear. Kim felt her shoulders relax, soothed by the intertwined melody of wind chimes, horses nickering, and songbirds.

A few minutes later, Kim arrived at the training arena where Lauren had been working with Speckles. Neither of them were there now. *She must have finished early.* Kim was so proud of Lauren's progress with Speckles. He was a different horse now—the once-ornery animal was now a gentle companion for Joey. Speckles would even tolerate a rub or a pat from the adult volunteers. Kim worried about his long-term care, knowing Speckles' knees would continue to deteriorate, but she was just as committed to keeping the wounded horse as Lauren was to working with him.

Kim walked to Gabe's field at the far end of the ranch before turning toward the round pen to begin the walk back. The unmistakable sound of a horse trotting stopped her. *Has one of the horses gotten out?* As she looked around, she spotted something, although it took her a minute to register what she was seeing. Lauren was standing on top of a picnic table with a lunge line attached to Speckles, who was circling the table.

"Whoa, Speckles. Stop," Lauren called out. Speckles obeyed.

"Good job, my speckled monster," Lauren said, ruffling the horse's mane. "You did great today."

"Well, lunging a horse from a picnic table is certainly something I've never seen before," Kim laughed as she approached.

Lauren's cheeks, already flushed from the sun, deepened a shade.

"I hope that was okay," she said, gathering the excess line in her hands. "He wasn't feeling the arena or the round pen, so I thought we'd try something new. For whatever reason, I think he likes me standing above him."

"I love it," Kim said. Lauren's methods were unconventional, but there was no doubt they worked. Speckles looked relaxed and happy.

"I was just going for a walk to clear my head," Kim explained. "But I certainly don't want to interrupt you two," she said, giving Speckles a good scratch behind the ears.

"You aren't interrupting at all. We were just winding down.

I'm trying to get this guy some exercise, see if we can keep his knees from locking up."

A loud whinny startled them. Joey. Speckles pawed at the ground and bobbed his head up and down, answering his impatient friend.

"Has Joey been like that the whole time you've been over here?"

"Yes, pretty much from the moment I took Speckles out," Lauren said. "Joey tried to follow us, and when I shut the gate he started pacing back and forth, sounding off every so often so we wouldn't forget he was waiting."

Lauren picked up a clump of clover and held it up to Speckles. "This guy will occasionally call to him to let him know all is well. It's so sweet."

What a relationship those two horses had formed. Kim had never seen anything quite like it.

"Keep doing what you're doing, Lauren. The methods may be unusual, but the results speak for themselves."

As Kim resumed her walk, Joey's pitiful cries drew her to paddock two. *Maybe I can be a temporary stand-in for Speckles.*

Joey's ears jerked forward at Kim's approach.

"Hey, bud," she said, entering the gate. "It's just me."

The horse greeted her with a quick sniff and then hurried to the gate, clearly waiting for his pasture-mate to come through it. After several minutes, Joey calmed down enough to join Kim by the water trough, his ears still pointed in Speckles' direction.

"Don't worry. He'll be back soon," Kim said, absentmindedly scratching Joey's back. She felt her stress and fear slowly fade away. *This is why I started this ministry: so hurting children could have an opportunity to simply be present with a horse.*

A memory of her beloved childhood horse, Country, flashed through her mind. How she had loved to spend time with her horse. Kim had owned several dogs, a cat, and a bunny, but there was nothing quite like earning the trust and respect of a thousand-pound animal. Or of having a horse mirror back to you how you were acting and feeling. Their ability to sense humans' moods and attitudes was uncanny, and yet somehow very comforting.

Joey turned his head toward Kim, and she looked deep into his eyes. How blessed they were to have this horse who had bonded with so many of the children. They loved helping to lead him from his paddock to the hitching post, where they brushed his spotted coat and assisted with cleaning his hooves. Yes, some children seemed scared that Joey couldn't see, but the majority of them adored Joey and were delighted to spend time with him.

Kim rubbed Joey's neck, and he leaned into her touch. *You are so trusting.* The blind faith he had in her and in those who cared for him was truly remarkable. She pulled at the collar of her T-shirt as a familiar fear swirled around her: What would happen to Joey, and all the other horses, if she had to close Hope Reins? Where would they go? After all, this place was the last hope for many of the horses. These weren't easy horses to rehome.

She would just have to find a way to keep things going.

Kim combed her fingers through Joey's short blond mane and began to pray out loud. "God, I have no idea how to make this work. I can't see how we are going to pay that pile of bills, or what would happen if we had to close our doors. But I truly believe you called me to start this ministry, and so I am choosing to trust you."

She leaned her head against Joey's shoulder. "I don't know how you are going to provide, but I am asking that you will—for

Joey and all the other horses, for the children, for our volunteers, for all those we will help in the future." She paused, then added, "Provide the money we need, provide the volunteers we need, provide the leadership qualities I need. God, please . . ."

A squeaky gate interrupted her prayer as Lauren let Speckles into the paddock. Immediately, Joey gave a joyful snort as he wheeled and ran to Speckles, nearly throwing Kim off-balance. The two friends bent their heads over each other's back in greeting, then eventually began to graze together.

"Don't worry, boys," Kim whispered. "I won't let you down. I promise. I am choosing to believe that God will provide . . . somehow."

CHAPTER 11

"Are you sure about this?" Sarah asked Lauren from her vantage point on Joey's back.

"You'll be fine," Lauren assured her. "Remember, he's done this many times before."

"Right, but he could see most of those other times!" Sarah retorted, suddenly regretting her offer to assess Joey's ability to carry a rider during sessions.

Things had been going just fine. Why had she decided to rock the boat?

Aly. As the little girl's face popped into her mind, Sarah knew she needed to go through with this. She had decided to ride bareback, which she always preferred. Besides, a saddle added more weight. A lighter load seemed the best plan for Joey's inaugural ride at Hope Reins.

Sarah had been working as Aly's session leader for the past

two months. Although the routine with Joey was pretty much the same from week to week, Sarah could sense Aly's trust in Joey building. She still hadn't said a word, but she was communicating much more to Sarah with her expressions. There was no question that Aly wanted to ride the horse she had come to love.

Sarah had discussed it with Kim, Barb, and Lauren shortly after Labor Day. They all agreed that it was time to take the next step with Joey. It would be so helpful if he could handle a rider, and the session leaders could have another horse to use.

Sarah had been excited with the decision until now. It had been so long since she had been on a horse that she wasn't sure she was the best candidate.

"You've got this, Sarah," Lauren said. "You have a ton of experience riding, and Joey has a ton of experience carrying a rider. Hold the reins loosely, and I'll lead him around the arena."

Lauren clucked her tongue and the trio began to move. The moment Sarah felt Joey's muscles move beneath her, her fear faded away. He moved so gracefully, so sure-footedly. *You're remarkable, Joey.* It was just a walk—and a slow one at that—but she was riding!

"How's it feel?" Lauren asked.

"Divine!" Sarah answered, feeling more free than she had in months.

Lauren led Joey around the arena three times before pronouncing him a natural. Sarah agreed completely. After the two women returned the tack to the shed and Joey to his field, they ran to tell Kim and Barb the good news: Joey was available to ride in sessions.

Two weeks later, Aly was back for another evening session. The five-year-old's gaze remained fixed on the ground as Sarah greeted her outside the office where the session leaders had met earlier to pray. Sarah had grown to appreciate those prayer times for the kids and the sessions. God seemed more than willing to answer those prayers.

But more than anything, Sarah wanted Aly to live with the exuberance that the other children couldn't contain as they laughed and ran around. Sarah believed the key for Aly was freeing her voice. Joey had begun to thrive, enjoying his life as a horse again. With his help, Sarah was convinced that Aly could learn to be a little girl again.

"Guess what?" Sarah said excitedly. "I have a surprise for you today."

Aly tried to peek behind Sarah's back, where she was clearly hiding something. "Ta-da!" Sarah whipped her hand in front of her, revealing a white riding helmet. "Joey would like to give you a ride!"

Aly's look, though guarded, was one of contained joy. Sarah could see the hint of a dimple forming in her cheek.

"So what do you say? You want to go for a ride?"

Aly nodded decisively. It was not her first time riding, just her first time on Joey. Sarah had made sure there were no surprises for Joey. She had saddled up Joey for a while yesterday, and he didn't mind at all. Now Sarah went through each step with Aly—putting on the saddle pad, saddle, and bridle, and attaching the reins. Out of the corner of her eye, Sarah could see that Aly was taking everything in. The little girl placed the helmet on her head but needed help fastening it under her chin. Once it was secure, Sarah handed Joey's lead rope to Aly.

"Go ahead and lead your horse. I'll walk right beside you."

Aly proudly led Joey to the round pen. They entered the small enclosure, and Sarah pointed to the four-step mounting block, which Aly used to get closer to Joey's back. Joey stood perfectly still as the young girl put her left boot in the left stirrup. Then Sarah lifted her up the rest of the way onto the saddle. Aly quickly found the right stirrup as she wiggled into position on the leather seat. Sarah handed the reins to Aly, showing her how to hold them loosely. Normally, the reins were attached to a bit bridle to control a horse, but Sarah had chosen a bitless bridle for Aly so that the little girl could use the reins to hold on to while Sarah controlled Joey with the lead line.

"Does everything feel okay?" Sarah asked, shortening up the stirrups.

Aly nodded her head. Sarah started Joey at a slow pace, and almost immediately an adorable toothless smile lit up Aly's face.

"Aly, I'm just going to walk Joey around the pen for a while. We want him to feel really comfortable in here. Since he can't see, he needs to be able to feel and hear where he is in the pen. The more we practice with him, the more he'll get used to it. I think he feels safe knowing that I'm leading him and that you are on his back."

Aly's brow was furrowed in concentration. Sarah admired the small rider's determination to help Joey learn his way around the pen. They had a job to do together. As they walked the inside perimeter of the pen, Sarah caught Cindy standing at the fence, watching her daughter ride. The look of joy on Cindy's face was rivaled only by Aly's.

Sarah was impressed by the young girl's riding posture—back straight, shoulders lowered, arms relaxed. *Textbook form.* Joey seemed eager to pick up the pace a little, so Sarah increased her speed by half walking, half jogging. After two trips around, sweat started to bead on her forehead and she was slightly out of breath, so Sarah slowed Joey to a walk again. *Could Joey be taught lunging without being able to see me?* She didn't know. That would be a challenge for another day.

Aly sat comfortably in the saddle, with a wide smile. "You are a very good rider, Aly," Sarah said as she helped her down at the end of the last lap and unstrapped her helmet. "Did you like that?"

Aly nodded enthusiastically.

"Let's take Joey over to the hitching post, so we can take the tack off and cool him down."

As Sarah loosened the cinch on the saddle, she kept talking. "Joey did well today too. I bet one day he might even be able to be ridden without someone having to lead him. What do you think?"

Aly's smile got even bigger.

"Well, big guy, Aly agrees. One day you are going to carry a rider all by yourself. What do you think about that?"

Joey nickered and stomped his foot. And a moment later, Sarah heard a small, whispered laugh.

Sarah and Aly led Joey back to his paddock, where Speckles was waiting.

"Let's go find your mom," Sarah said, smiling as Aly's hand raised in a timid good-bye wave to Joey.

Cindy met them halfway to the office and gave Aly a big hug. Sarah could tell Aly welcomed the embrace.

"You went for a ride on Joey!" Cindy exclaimed, picking her

daughter up and swinging her around. "How was it? Did Joey do a good job?"

As Cindy lowered Aly back to the ground, Sarah hoped the little girl would tell her mother about her ride, if for no other reason than to hear her voice.

A nod was the only answer given. Although Aly's bright eyes showed her excitement, Sarah was disappointed. Still, she tried to focus on what the little girl had just accomplished.

"Aly and Joey both did a great job. Aly is a natural in the saddle, and Joey really trusts her." Sarah bent down to look Aly in the eye. "I am so proud of you."

Aly looked up at her mother, her eyes shining with delight.

Cindy twirled her daughter's ponytail. "Oh, Aly, I am so proud of you too."

The little girl whispered something to her mom. Cindy laughed and gave her a little squeeze. "Yes, I am proud of Joey, too. He is a very good horse."

Sarah was glad the session went well and was overjoyed that Aly had gotten to ride Joey. *She's connecting well with Joey.* Shy as Aly was, she was caring for him and building trust with him. Sarah knew from experience how long of a process building trust could be.

CHAPTER 12

"KIM, THERE SIMPLY ISN'T enough money to keep things going past next month," said Allin. Barb's husband glanced at the other board members sitting in Kim and Mike's family room before continuing.

"Aside from charging for sessions—" Allin put his hand up before Kim could protest. She closed her mouth and tried to relax while Allin had the floor. "Aside from charging for sessions, which I know you are strongly against, and I respect that, a fund-raiser—and a fund-raiser sooner than later—is the only way to get the influx of cash the ranch needs."

Kim straightened up. "Okay," she began. "I know that we need to think about holding a major event. But it takes money to make money. Money that we don't actually have. Where would we even begin? Our kickoff event was certainly not cheap, and we were constantly worried about the weather, remember?" She glanced at Lori, who together with Kim had almost worn out her weather app during the weeks leading up to that grand opening.

"Maybe we can hold it off the ranch?" Lori suggested. "We could contact different venues to see if they would consider donating space. If they hear about the ministry, they might be open to that. And then we wouldn't have to worry about the weather."

"Possibly someone might be willing to cut us a deal on catering," added Kathy, a retired psychologist and friend of Lori's.

Ben, a friend and work colleague of Mike's, stood up from the love seat to stretch. "It would be nice to have photographs of the horses and ranch to show the people who come, to give them an idea of what you all do."

Ideas, suggestions, and possibilities were tossed around for the next twenty minutes. With each one, Kim's fear and frustration built, until her head began to throb. Finally, Allin called for the meeting to be adjourned. "But I encourage each one of you to pray during the week for wisdom about this matter. See you next week."

Kim certainly prayed. In fact, she felt as though she prayed for little else that week. She researched fund-raising ideas, discussed various ideas and thoughts with friends not associated with the ranch, and made countless lists of possibilities. Nothing like a list to bring order to chaos! But there was no order to be found.

Each place she called was sympathetic to her situation and inspired by the ministry, but they were all either booked solid through the holidays or unable to lower the prices. It was mid-November, and she was competing with company events that had been planned at least a year before.

And even if a venue opened up, would anyone want to donate so close to Christmas? The odds were not looking good.

With the follow-up board meeting scheduled the next evening, Kim sat in the Hope Reins office, looking at a sheet of paper in front of her. It was the list of possible venues, every one with a line through it. "Lord, why are you being so silent? Why would you bring us this far only to let us lose it all?" Kim prayed her lament out loud.

The ranch was quiet, now that the last volunteers had left. Kim tossed her pen on the table and got up. *Time to walk.* The sun seemed to be setting rapidly; the time change meant there were no more evening sessions until the spring. They couldn't conduct sessions in the dark.

Grateful for the warmer-than-usual weather, Kim headed straight for paddock two without even thinking. Joey had that effect on people, drawing them like a magnet. A moment later she was beside the handsome black-and-white horse, who was standing near the hay box.

"Hey, Joey," Kim announced her presence, certain that the intuitive horse already knew she was there.

She rubbed her hand along his side, lingering on several of his spots.

"How are you, baby?" she asked, a lump rising in her throat at the thought of what would happen to the blind horse if they couldn't figure out a way to raise the needed funds.

She looked across the paddock to Speckles. He was just starting to make real progress. What would happen to him? Who would want to care for him? Each of the Hope Reins horses was her responsibility.

As her anxiety began to rise, Kim forced herself to breathe

in through her nose and out through her mouth. Her fingers began to tingle. *Slow down and sit down. But where?* A late afternoon drizzle had left the ground muddy between the piles of manure. *Back to the office?* Just the thought of it made her heart rate quicken. And then . . . it dawned on her: Joey and Speckles' hay box. She climbed in, sat cross-legged, and closed her eyes.

Inhale.

Exhale.

Inhale.

Exhale.

Suddenly a large nose pushed against her cheek. Oh! She opened her eyes and stared at Joey, who was intent on finding out what large, delicious treat was in his feedbox.

"Sorry, boy," Kim apologized, reaching out to stroke his chin. "Hope you don't mind."

She gave the curious horse a handful of hay, which he eagerly took. She absently stroked his upper leg as he chewed.

"What is going to happen to you if I can't figure this out? What's going to happen to all of you? To the kids? To this place?" A tear made its way down her cheek. "You are doing so well here, Joey. You connected with Ethan and little Aly. You've been a friend to Speckles, and—" she turned to look at him—"you've provided such comfort to me. If only people could see what you do, what goes on here, and get a glimpse of true hope, then maybe . . ." Her words trailed off, crowded out by an idea.

Have it here.

The words were not audible, but they were extremely clear.

Have what here? Kim pondered for a moment. *The fundraiser? But how? It would cost too much. It's getting cold. It might rain. It's getting too close to Christmas.*

And yet, in spite of every reason she threw out for why it wouldn't work, she felt a flood of peace wash over her. While sitting in the hay box, Kim began to talk it out with Joey.

"Well, what if we did have it here? It would definitely give people a chance to see firsthand what we do. We wouldn't have to pay anything for the space. We could ask volunteers and board members to bring food, and even do s'mores in the fire pit. We could reuse a lot of the kickoff event decorations and ask people for the rest. The only thing we can't control," she said, looking at the sun dipping below the tree line, "is the weather."

Joey reached around her to grab another mouthful of hay, which got Speckles' attention. He warily approached the hay box, not too sure about joining this party. Kim watched the dynamics of the two. The trust they had built with each other was astounding.

Trust.

The word seemed to float in front of Kim, like a feather waiting to be snatched in midair.

It was a concept Kim wrestled with daily. But what other choice did she have? If God was leading them to have the fundraiser at the ranch, then she would just have to trust him to control all the things she couldn't.

There was no denying that he had proven himself pretty trustworthy so far.

"We can do this," Allin said, sitting at Kim and Mike's kitchen table the next evening. The board members were enjoying the cookies Lori had brought. "Sure, it's a little risky with the weather and all, but we can always plan for a rain date and advertise it as a casual fund-raising dinner/Christmas party."

"We could put Santa hats on the horses," Kathy suggested with a laugh.

"I love it!" Kim exclaimed.

The ideas flowed nonstop for the next hour. Lists were made and assignments handed out. Kim, who had been dreading the idea of a large-scale fund-raiser, found this new idea both exciting and manageable. There was no doubt in her mind that it would be fun. But would it be a success? Would they raise all the money they needed to keep the ranch going?

CHAPTER 13

"COME BACK, YOU BIG OL' THIEF!" Lauren yelled as she chased after Speckles.

The horse, obviously experiencing some reprieve from pain, galloped away from her at full speed, carrying something in his teeth.

This was not the first time she'd had to chase him down. Several months earlier, he had taken off with a rake that had been left behind in his field. He had looked ridiculous running through the paddock with it in his mouth. It had taken Lauren forever to catch him.

Last month, he had snatched a burlap wreath—adorned with various-shaped gourds—off the tack shed door. The tempting Thanksgiving-themed decoration was irresistible. Thankfully, Lauren had been holding his lead line at the time, so he didn't get very far with the booty.

But this was a different story. Speckles had added vandalism to his rap sheet—he had a truck's side-view mirror clenched between his teeth!

The mirror had been dangling from a volunteer's truck, temporarily duct-taped in place. Obviously, the tape had lost its stickiness. Lauren hadn't noticed it when she and Speckles were taking their usual morning walk. But someone else did.

Speckles seemed to love these walks—the unhurried pace, the meandering paths, the time alone. It was evident that Speckles enjoyed Joey's companionship, and yet the blind horse did place a lot of demands on Speckles—constant nickering to ascertain where Speckles was located, a lack of concern for personal space, and nervous pacing during storms. Lauren had come to realize that even the most patient of caregivers needed a break every once in a while. As much as he loved Joey, Speckles was no exception.

Lauren had allowed Speckles to lead the way this morning, and he quickly wandered over to the miniature horses, Hope and Josie. Technically, *wander* wasn't the right word. Speckles all but dragged Lauren over to their pen. Lauren suspected her boy had a bit of a crush on Josie, but unfortunately for him, his love went unrequited. After ignoring Speckles' wooing rituals—teeth baring, tail raising, and compulsive neighing—Josie moved to the other side of her pen. Dejected by her lack of interest, Speckles sauntered over to the parking lot, where he sniffed at the gravel, picked at some leaves, and then reached up and tore the mirror off!

Duct tape has a distinctive sound when it is ripped, and it got Lauren's attention. When she realized what Speckles had done, she dropped the lead rope and tried to gently take the mirror from Speckles' mouth. That was when he bolted. For a horse with significant knee problems, he could move surprisingly fast. And Lauren, struggling with her own knee problems that day, was no match for the horse.

Speckles ran toward the round pen, then veered right and headed toward his paddock to show Joey his most recent plunder. He stopped by the gate and gave a muffled snort, impeded by the large mirror between his lips. The message, however, was clearly understood by Joey, who trotted right over to him to investigate the strange object in his buddy's mouth.

That's when Lauren made her move.

"Gotcha," Lauren panted, placing a hand on Speckles' back, before bending over to catch her breath. "You . . ." she said, rubbing his side, "are one fast thief."

Speckles looked at her defiantly. To keep him from bolting again, Lauren quickly pulled a treat out of her pocket.

"Trade you the mirror for a carrot?" she suggested, wagging the treat under his mouth.

Speckles turned his head away, as if attempting to resist her temptation. But finally his stomach won out and he dropped the mirror into Lauren's hand.

A shredded remnant of tape hung limply from the damp, smudged mirror. Lauren gave it a quick once-over. Other than some horse slobber, it seemed no worse for wear following its romp around the ranch.

The owner of the truck, a feeding volunteer, had heard all the commotion and came over.

"Um, did Speckles just . . . ?" he started to ask.

Lauren sheepishly held up the mirror. "I am so sorry," she replied, trying hard not to laugh.

The volunteer took the mirror from Lauren and burst out laughing. His loud guffaw turned the culprit's head.

"Serves me right for being too cheap to get it fixed the first time," he chuckled.

Grateful for his laid-back attitude, Lauren wished she had the money to pay for a new mirror, but her own car was one repair away from being held together with duct tape!

A sense of humor was definitely a necessary requirement for working with horses. Hopefully, the man would get the mirror fixed or use some stronger duct tape. Or park farther away next time!

Thanks to Speckles' escapade, Lauren was out of breath and her knees were throbbing. "Speckles, I have to cut the walk short this morning." When Speckles rejoined Joey, the two handsome boys made their way to the far side of the paddock, near where some mares were grazing in the adjacent field. The Appaloosa geldings seemed to fancy themselves quite the ladies' men with their heads held high and tails up, prancing back and forth.

Good grief. Lauren chuckled to herself. *What a pair.*

Lauren was headed back to the tack shed to return the lead rope when she saw Sarah pull into the parking lot.

"Hey there!" Lauren called out.

"Hey, yourself," Sarah said. "What in the world have you been up to?"

"Oh, Speckles was up to his old tricks again this morning. Would you believe he tore a side-view mirror off a truck?"

"You're kidding!" Sarah laughed. "He's becoming quite the accomplished kleptomaniac, isn't he?"

"And a fast one too," Lauren replied. "He ran me all over the ranch. I could barely keep up with him. If he hadn't stopped to show his prize to Joey, I'd probably still be chasing him."

The two women made their way over to paddock two and leaned against the gate to watch Joey and Speckles graze.

"Will you look at that?" Sarah said, pointing to a shiny object nestled in the grass at the base of the gate. "I swear, those wind chimes spend more time on the ground than they do on the fence." She reached through the gate to snag the fallen chime.

Lauren recognized it immediately. "That one is Speckles' favorite," she said, twirling the little ceramic frog sitting atop a lily pad. "He loves to bump it with his nose and make it jingle when we walk around the paddock." She paused for a moment. "Funny, though, I could have sworn that one was hanging way over there."

That's when they noticed it. There, lying on the ground about twenty feet from the hay box, were about fifteen wind chimes in a type of zigzag line.

"How did that happen?" Sarah asked. She and Lauren looked at each other. "Speckles!" they blurted out simultaneously.

"You rascal," Lauren called out to Speckles. "You're the one who's been taking these down, aren't you?" Speckles nickered and shook his head.

"Don't try to deny it," Lauren teased.

It all makes sense now. The mouthy horse, irresistible dangling items, and a pasture-mate to impress with his plunder.

"Should we put them back up?" Sarah asked.

"I'm not sure we need to," said Lauren, suddenly seeing the truth clearly for the first time—Joey didn't need the chimes anymore. Speckles, the reformed bully of a horse couldn't participate in sessions or do many things the other horses could, but he had an important job.

A tear trickled down her cheek.

"Speckles has become Joey's eyes," she whispered reverently to Sarah.

Sarah glanced at Lauren, then looked at Joey. "And Joey's

become his purpose," she added, her voice overcome with emotion.

The women stood together silently for several minutes, watching the two spotted horses. As they turned back to do their chores, a searching nicker reverberated through the air, quickly followed by an answering neigh.

Lauren smiled. *I will never grow tired of hearing that.*

CHAPTER 14

Kɪᴍ ꜱᴛᴏᴏᴅ ꜰᴀᴄɪɴɢ ᴛʜᴇ Hope Reins office, trying to assess whether the fresh pine wreath she had hung on the door was straight. After making a slight adjustment, she turned around to take in the whole beautiful scene. *Just like a Hallmark Christmas movie.*

A huge canvas sign bearing the words "Merry Christmas— Love, Hope Reins" greeted visitors as they arrived. A large cypress Christmas tree stood just outside the office, and pic- nic tables were laden with candy canes, Christmas cookies, the ingredients for s'mores, and hot chocolate. Two-foot-tall plastic candy canes lined the walkways, bright red bows adorned the trees, and wreaths made of fresh pine and magnolia branches tied with burlap ribbon hung on each of the storage shed doors. There was also a large wooden star suspended by wire between two trees near the fire pit. Stockings, personalized with each horse's name, hung from the gate on each paddock, and every hitching post was wrapped in garland.

"Can you believe this? We actually pulled this all together in less than a month, and for such a small amount of money," Kim said to Barb, unable to contain her exuberance. "And, the weather is perfect! Not a raindrop in sight and the mildest temperatures I can recall in December." God had provided, and she was still in awe.

"Are *you* ready?" Barb asked, her face beaming with excitement and hope.

Am I ready? Will I ever be truly ready to ask people for money? Taking care of horses? Sure. Helping kids find hope through a relationship with a horse? Telling them about Jesus? Absolutely. But asking people for money so they could keep doing those things? Not so much.

"I don't think I have much choice, do I?" Kim said, trying to keep her tone light. "I just pray we will raise enough to keep us going for a few more months. I can't even think about the alternative."

Barb squeezed her hand. "Sweetie, try to relax. You've invited some great potential donors and reached out to some wonderful people who have already given generously to the ministry and will likely do so again when they hear the families' stories. You have turned this ranch into a Christmas wonderland. It's going to be a terrific afternoon."

Kim had been excited about the guest list, which included many generous past donors, all the volunteers and families receiving services at Hope Reins, pastors and leaders from several local churches, a news reporter from WRAL, and even the lieutenant governor of North Carolina.

But will they support our cause? she lamented silently.

Trust.

The word again drifted through her mind. She had trusted God with the weather. Surely she could trust him with the donations. Yet at the moment, weather seemed a far easier request.

As Barb headed over to the refreshment table for a final check, Kim decided to use the last few minutes before the first guests arrived to go and check on Joey, who had recently had all of his wind chimes taken down in the paddock. Kim missed the cheerful tingle of the chimes, but the truth was, Joey didn't need them anymore.

"Well, look at you, Mr. No More Wind Chimes," Kim called out to Joey, who was standing near the water trough. "You've really come a long way, haven't you? And you," she said, calling louder to Speckles, who had moved as far away as he could from the increasing noise and activity. "You make one special companion."

Kim scratched Joey between his ears. "Lord," she prayed aloud, leaning into the horse who brought her such comfort and strength, "if it's your will, please let us keep doing this. Please let Hope Reins continue. And Lord, please, please help me trust you more."

The cheerful voice of Brenda Lee singing "Rockin' Around the Christmas Tree" was the signal that the festivities were about to begin.

Kim gave Joey one more good scratch and took a deep breath. "I'll see you later."

A chorus of voices yelled "Cheese!" in unison as Mike snapped a picture.

Kim, Lauren, Barb, Jo Anne, Sarah, and several other volunteers had all crowded around Joey for a photo. Joey had been transformed into a holiday horse with a bright Santa hat, and he reveled in the extra attention.

A line of guests, mostly small children, had formed in front of his paddock, all eager to get their picture taken with the Appaloosa in festive attire. Young faces lit up with joy, and there were squeals of delight when Mark, one of the training volunteers, fed Joey a carrot. Joey really loved his carrots!

Ornaments were being decorated at the craft tables to be added to the Hope Reins tree. Other horses wearing Santa hats were having their pictures taken, too, in the common area.

Everything seems to be running smoothly. Kim felt her shoulders relax slightly as Mike gave her a hug. She had wanted this afternoon to be a sweet time of celebration and fun, and that was exactly what was transpiring.

Static from the borrowed sound system got their attention, then Hank's voice announced that it was time for the horses to be returned to their fields and all the guests to head over to the Christmas tree.

Kim's shoulders tensed again. She had been secretly dreading this part.

"Looks like you're up," Mike whispered in her ear, then kissed her on the forehead. "You've got this, Kim. Just speak from your heart."

She wished she shared Mike's confidence or could even ask him to make the remarks. But the fact was she *had* to do this. How would people know about all the amazing things Hope Reins did if she didn't tell them? How would they know what to give—why to give—if she didn't tell them? God had given her this ministry, and she couldn't pick and choose what she did and did not want to do for this endeavor.

Guests quickly took seats around the large cypress tree that had been transformed with Christmas lights, popcorn garlands, and wooden ornaments painted and hung by the children earlier in the afternoon. Kim glanced at the assembled crowd. She had greeted each person as they arrived, noticing many familiar faces—volunteers, board members, church friends, neighbors, members of Bay Leaf Baptist Church, and Dr. Gallagher. But there were also countless people who were first-time visitors at Hope Reins.

"I am so excited to be able to welcome you to the first-ever Hope Reins Christmas Celebration and Fund-Raiser. We are so blessed and grateful to have you here. Just a year and a half ago, this ranch was little more than an idea. But thanks to the tireless dedication and generosity of many of the people gathered here today—champions who have stepped up in faith because they wanted to make a difference—Hope Reins has become a reality."

A small round of applause broke out, led by Barb, Lauren, and Sarah. Behind them, Mike smiled, clapped, and nodded in support. Kim took a deep, steadying breath before continuing.

"Our mission at Hope Reins is to pair a horse with a hurting child, to help open that child's heart. But our cause is not just kids and horses. Hope Reins is based upon 2 Corinthians 1:3-5, which explains that God comforts us in our time of need, so that we can comfort others in their time of need. That's what Hope Reins is all about —providing comfort and healing for others, just as God provides for us."

Kim's voice grew stronger with every word.

"That comfort is not reserved just for the hurting children and their families, though. It is freely offered to our volunteers, to people who come for a tour, and to every person who donates their time, their energy, and, yes, their money. We consider everyone who walks up our driveway and contributes to our cause a member of the Hope Reins family—because that's what we are." She looked directly at the small cluster of volunteers standing right up front.

Another round of applause erupted. Behind the gathered crowd, Joey whinnied and stomped his foot, momentarily drawing attention away from Kim, who welcomed the opportunity to clear her throat.

"Yes, Joey, I'm getting to you," Kim joked.

"You'll notice I said the word *freely* a moment ago," she continued. "There's a reason for that. Just as the comfort and healing of Jesus is offered freely, the services at Hope Reins are offered 100 percent free of charge to the families we serve. Many of our families would not be able to afford this kind of personalized service, and so from the very beginning, we were determined that no family would be asked to pay for their child to visit Hope Reins, and we want to keep it that way."

Kim looked around the crowd, her gaze falling on several of the families they served. Sitting in the back was Marcus, the first child to ever participate in a session at Hope Reins. Since Marcus had been in foster care for years, Kim had been delighted to see him form a strong bond with Gabe. To Kim's right was Ella, a sweet seven-year-old who had become withdrawn following the death of her baby sister. Her mom told Kim that for weeks, the only time Ella would smile was when she was with Josie, whose small size provided Ella with an opportunity to tenderly care for her as she no longer could for her sister.

To Kim's left was Andrew, a shy boy of eleven who had discovered a friend in Shiloh, who was also slow to warm up to people. The two built trust in each other and loved to play soccer together in the arena. Andrew's dad reported that he had even made a new friend at school recently and attributed that to Andrew's sessions with Shiloh. And sitting right in front of Kim were Cindy and Aly. Kim's throat tightened at the image of mother and daughter, still waiting for their breakthrough moment. Still hoping for healing. Kim couldn't help but wink at Cindy, hoping the gesture conveyed her admiration for the woman.

"I would very much like to introduce you to one of the families we are privileged to serve. Please meet Ellen and Christine."

Kim extended her hand to fourteen-year-old Christine and her mother. She put her arm around Christine. "These beautiful ladies have agreed to share some of their story with you all today, so I am going to turn the microphone over to them."

Kim took a few steps back as Ellen began to share from a sheet of paper, which shook ever so slightly in her grip.

"After moving to Raleigh from Long Island following a difficult divorce, I noticed that Christine began having a hard time. She was anxious, fearful, and closed off. At first I thought it was normal teenage stuff, but she just kept retreating further and further from me." Ellen glanced at her daughter, and Christine nodded silent permission to continue.

"It wasn't until I discovered the scars on her arms that I realized we had a real problem. My beautiful baby girl was cutting herself." Christine looked down. Her mother grabbed hold of her hand.

"We began seeing a therapist to address some of the issues Christine was facing—things like abandonment and depression. But the therapist also recommended additional therapy—specifically equine therapy, which she said would give Christine a chance to practice social interactions in a nonthreatening environment. She gave us information about Hope Reins."

Ellen's eyes filled with tears. "I cannot begin to tell you what a huge impact this place has made on my daughter—and on me. The moment Christine stepped out of the car, it was like she had come home. She met all the horses but seemed to have this instant connection to Deetz, who had just recently come to the ranch."

Christine smiled at the mention of her favorite horse.

"She began talking to Deetz while she groomed him. She worked hard to build trust with him so she could ride him. She even asked if she could help clean up the manure in his pasture."

Ellen glanced at Kim. "It's as if by caring for Deetz, Christine was learning to care for herself. And as she learned to care for herself, she—we—discovered there's a God who cares deeply for us."

She looked toward the sky for a brief moment before resuming. "However, for a single mom with serious health problems, money is tight. We would not be here if not for those of you who give to make this all possible." Ellen squeezed her daughter's hand once again. "We both thank you and urge you to keep giving."

Kim's heart soared as she hugged Ellen and Christine and thanked them for sharing their story.

"Well, folks, I couldn't have said that any better. I mean, that is why we are here and why we do what we do. Your donations make all of that possible."

Kim motioned to Pastor Jacumin. "I want to acknowledge the incredible generosity of the church who provided the land around you. Because of this benefactor, we pay next to nothing for this beautiful property. And I want to thank a loyal group of volunteers who feed the horses twice a day, help run sessions, do minor repairs, and load wheelbarrows full of poop each week.

But caring for horses is not cheap, and even more so for us because more than half of our horses are dealing with the effects of abuse and neglect."

She pointed to Joey. "Horses like our Joey, who was left permanently blind because of horrible neglect."

Kim heard several gasps from the audience. "He has found a second chance here at Hope Reins, but he and his pasture-mate, Speckles, who has a similar heartbreaking story, both require specialized care. Add to that the cost of maintaining a ranch, and it all adds up."

Lord, please provide, she silently prayed.

"We would be honored if you would be willing to join our cause—to partner with us through making a donation. Would you prayerfully consider supporting us financially? If so, stop by the commitment table and consider the ways you might be able to help. Please enjoy the rest of the afternoon. Spend some time with the horses and help yourselves to the refreshments."

After Kim closed in prayer, the guests began to disperse, and she exhaled deeply. Mike made his way through the crowd.

"You did good, babe," he said, enveloping her in a warm hug.

"I hope it was enough."

"Come on," Mike said. "The hard part's over. Get on out there and enjoy yourself. You've earned it." He kissed the tip of her nose as Joey whinnied and nickered behind them.

"Besides, your boyfriend's waiting for you."

Kim saw a good crowd gathered around the commitment table as she made her way over to Joey's paddock.

A man, a woman, and a young boy stood near the fence. The little boy, who appeared to be around seven or eight, was holding his hands over his ears and rocking back and forth on his heels.

The woman knelt down in front of him and began to speak, but the boy pushed her away. The man seemed to be looking for the easiest escape route. Kim was conflicted. Should she walk over to greet them, or would they rather be left alone? *Well,* she reasoned, *you did just say everyone here is family.* She smiled as she approached the trio. A flash of embarrassment crossed the woman's face before being replaced with a bright smile.

"Hi, I'm Kim. Welcome to Hope Reins. I'm glad you came out today."

"I'm Rebekah," the woman said, "and this is my husband, James, and our son, Nathan." She put her hands on her son's shoulders, but he immediately pushed them off.

The boy flung his head to the right, rubbing his cheek on his shoulder, and made several unintelligible sounds before turning away from the adults to stare at Joey and Speckles.

Kim looked at the parents. "How did you hear about us?"

"A friend invited us to come today. You have really helped her daughter, and she thought that maybe . . ." Rebekah's words trailed off as she gazed at her son.

A rousing rendition of "Jingle Bells" erupted near the Christmas tree.

Nathan cupped his hands over his ears and began rocking forcefully back and forth.

"We should probably get Nathan home," James said apologetically.

He looked at his wife. Rebekah's expression was a mixture of sadness and defeat. It was clear she had hoped for a different experience here. Kim's heart went out to her. It was obvious that their son had some kind of special need, most likely autism. Kim smiled at the boy and asked, "Has Nathan ever seen a horse up close?"

Rebekah shook her head.

"Would he like to?"

Rebekah knelt down in front of her son. "Nathan, would you like to see a horse?"

Nathan shook his head wildly and made a guttural sound. Rebekah, however, did not seem the least bit deterred.

"Nathan," she repeated, extending her finger in front of the boy's face, then slowly pointing toward Joey. "See the horse?"

Nathan's eyes followed his mother's finger.

"Hoorr!" Nathan shouted, noticing the large animal.

His hazel eyes widened a moment, then he jumped up. The indifference of a moment ago had been instantly replaced with unfiltered joy.

The power of a horse, Kim thought with gratitude.

"That's Joey."

"Nathan, can you say hi to Joey?"

Nathan opened and closed his fist in Joey's direction. "Hh-iiiee," he said.

Joey was standing about twenty feet away, but Kim was confident he knew he was being watched.

Kim gave Rebekah and James a quick rundown of Joey's past and how he came to Hope Reins. Joey's large head was tilted to the side—he seemed to be listening in.

"How does he make his way around the field?" James asked.

Kim explained the accident with the fencing, the solution with the wind chimes, and now the unique relationship Joey had formed with Speckles.

"Speckles herds Joey around the paddock like a border collie."

"Wow, so Speckles is like a seeing-eye horse for Joey," Rebekah said, smiling.

"He really is," Kim said. *What would we have done without you, Speckles?*

James crouched down next to Nathan. "Hey, buddy. Ms. Kim just told us that Joey can't see. He's blind. That means his eyes don't work."

Nathan squeezed his eyes shut. "Daark! Hoorrss, daark."

He's trying to put himself in Joey's place.

"Nathan," Kim said, delighted when the boy glanced at her, "Joey can't see, but he knows you're here. Do you want him to come over so you can touch him?"

"Noo-noo. Noo-noo!" the boy shouted, violently shaking his head.

Kim stood up. "I'm so sorry," she said, unsure of what she had said wrong, and feeling awful for upsetting him.

"It's okay," Rebekah assured her. "Nathan has a sensory processing disorder and doesn't like being touched. I think he assumes no one else does either." James began talking softly into Nathan's ear.

"His autism and sensory problems cause him to withdraw, making social interaction very difficult." The soft-spoken mother expressed great sorrow over her son's lack of friends. He seemed not to have the interest or ability to connect with anyone.

"I worry so much about what kind of life he is going to have," she admitted.

Nathan walked up to the fence and squeezed the top rail until his knuckles turned white.

Rebekah lowered her voice as she added, "More than anything, I just want to connect with my son."

James put his arm around his wife, and she leaned her head

on his shoulder. The two watched their son observing the horses. *I can't even imagine not being able to hug my children,* Kim found herself thinking.

Speckles walked up to Joey, and when Joey tried to nuzzle his pasture-mate, Speckles snapped at Joey as if to say, *Not in the mood.* Joey stepped away, giving Speckles the space he needed.

Just as Speckles had figured out Joey's limitations, Joey had figured out Speckles'. The two stood several feet apart, heads lowered over the thinning grass.

Nathan started reciting what sounded like lines from a movie or TV show. He spoke so clearly that it surprised Kim. Apparently, reciting lines came much easier to him than spontaneous conversation. As the boy was speaking, there was another surprise. Speckles began walking toward Nathan. *What is he up to?*

Now it was time for Speckles to be introduced to the family. "Speckles came to us at the same time as Joey. Sadly, he also has a history of abuse and abandonment. We discovered shortly after getting him that he is in pain almost every day, so much so that he can't be ridden. But he definitely has a purpose here."

"He's Joey's eyes," Rebekah whispered.

"Yes, he is."

Speckles walked closer to Nathan. The boy stared at the speckled horse as he approached, yet Nathan never moved—his hands continued to grip the fence rail. Speckles stopped in front of the boy. Then, as if in slow motion, he lowered his brown-and-white head over Nathan's hand. The boy jerked his hand away, looking as if he were going to cry.

Speckles abruptly flicked his head to the side, and Kim began to approach him to gently shoo him away. But before she could take a second step, Nathan put his hand back on the rail.

James held up his hand in a "let's see what happens" gesture.

Speckles again lowered his head toward the boy. This time the boy reached his right index finger out and delicately touched Speckles right above the nostrils.

"Noosse," he said dragging out each sound.

Kim heard Rebekah gasp. "Yes, that is Speckles' nose," she commended. "Speckles has owies," she added cautiously. "He doesn't like big touches."

Big touches. I like that wording.

Nathan pulled his hand away and stepped back. Speckles leaned his head over the fence in search of the boy. Kim had never seen Speckles seek out a child like this before. Nathan once again reached up and touched the same spot on Speckles.

The horse blew a puff of air onto Nathan's finger. The boy immediately pulled his hand away. Rebekah tensed up, and Kim prepared herself for the boy's scream. But instead she heard what sounded a lot like a seal bark. *He's laughing!*

Rebekah grabbed her husband's hand as her son leaned into Speckles and blew on the horse. Speckles answered with a snort. Nathan mimicked the sound.

What was happening?

The magnitude of the moment was almost more than Kim could process. Horse and boy stood facing each other for several minutes as if communicating something profound that only the two of them understood. Eventually, Joey nickered impatiently, and Speckles sauntered over to him. The spell broken, Rebekah dropped to her knees in front of her son.

"You touched Speckles," she said with breathless wonder. "You are so brave."

Nathan tilted his head to the side and looked at his mother as if seeing her for the first time. Tentatively, he reached out his right index finger and touched her nose.

Kim wanted to shout a prayer of thanksgiving, but instead she and James stood transfixed, afraid to make a sound.

Nathan was still studying his mother, his finger still on her nose. A hint of a smile formed on Rebekah's lips as she exhaled a short puff of air on Nathan's finger. He instantly jerked his hand away.

Rebekah's face fell.

But a moment later, Nathan put his finger up to his own nose and exhaled. He reached for his mother's nose again, and she exhaled for the second time. Nathan did not pull away. Instead, the young boy threw his head back and laughed his barking chortle.

Rebecca raised one finger and cautiously moved it toward her son's nose.

The boy started to duck, but Rebekah stopped and asked, "Mama's finger touch Nathan's nose?"

Nathan cast a glance at Speckles before turning back to his mother and bending his head toward her. The touch was gentle and delicate. Nathan responded with a forceful, but joyful, exhale. Kim didn't know if she should laugh or cry. Both seemed appropriate reactions to the miracle she had just witnessed.

Delight—a look of sheer love—shone from Rebekah's face. Her eyes were riveted on her son, her face flushed with emotion, her neck red and splotchy. Kim couldn't remember ever seeing someone look lovelier.

She looked at the two horses in the paddock, who had no way of understanding the gift they had just given this family. Two horses that many would say were broken and unusable had just brought hope into the life of a mother desperate to reach her son.

Kim hugged Rebekah and James and urged them to visit the ranch again, before she joined the fun of making s'mores.

"That was really something," said Debra, the woman from WRAL. She had been standing near Joey's gate when Nathan started interacting with the horses.

"It really was," Kim agreed, still moved by what had just happened.

"I take it that kind of thing happens a lot out here?" Debra asked.

"It really does. Not always in such an intense or immediate manner. But real change happens here. I just pray it will continue."

Debra's eyes crinkled as she smiled. "Well, maybe a little publicity might help. I'll be in touch."

As the last of the guests left, Kim headed to the commitment table, where Barb was frantically pecking away on a calculator. In front of her were several neatly stacked piles of five-, ten-, and twenty-dollar bills, dozens of checks, and an enormous stack of commitment cards.

"Oh my goodness!" Kim gasped. "Is all of that . . . ?"

"Yes ma'am. Enough to keep us going for at least another year!"

"Seriously?" Kim's heart began to flutter. First Nathan and Rebekah, and now this.

Overwhelmed at God's provision, Kim started to cry. Had it only been four weeks ago that she had sat with Joey and feared losing him and all the other horses? So much had changed in such a short amount of time, and yet in the back of her mind, she still wondered if it would be enough. It was a constant battle.

Walking in blind faith is not for wimps.

CHAPTER 15

ONE DAY A FEW WEEKS LATER, Lauren arrived for her normal training time with Speckles. His pain had increased so much that he simply couldn't handle more than a once-a-week work-out. After getting her two girls set up at a picnic table to work on their math assignment, she headed to the tack shed.

What a beautiful day to be training my favorite horse! The noonday sun had chased lingering clouds away. Lauren glanced at her watch as she headed toward paddock two. Sarah was due in about ten minutes to work with Joey.

The women had decided to try training both horses during the same time frame, hoping the dual session would help to ease some of Joey's separation anxiety. Although Joey's training really just consisted of walking him around the arena or round pen, it was still important to work with the horse in settings outside of his field.

Debra from WRAL had been true to her word. A recent article about Hope Reins had been posted on the station's website, with a picture of Joey in his Santa hat. Inquiries about sessions had increased, with many callers specifically requesting to meet the handsome Appaloosa.

"Hey, boys!" Lauren called out, opening the gate. "Are you ready for some fun?"

Joey came trotting right over, but Speckles didn't move. His stance seemed awkward, his eyes wide. *He's hurting a lot today.* Joey followed Lauren to his tense pasture-mate.

"Hey, speckled monster," she said, approaching slowly. "What's up? Not feeling good?"

Speckles snorted. He pinned his ears back, moved them forward, then pinned them back again. The motion reminded Lauren of her oldest daughter's habit of opening and closing the refrigerator door while trying to decide on a snack.

Speckles held his back leg slightly off the ground and eyed Lauren warily, seeing the halter in her hand.

"It's okay, bud," she said, dropping the halter on the ground. "Let's just hang out."

Lauren knew that any movement would help Speckles loosen his joints and hopefully alleviate some pain. But she had also spent enough time with him to know that if he thought she expected something from him, he would dig in his heels and refuse to move. *Where's a hanging side mirror when you need one? That would surely get him moving.*

Lauren stood between Joey and Speckles, trying to formulate a plan. As she deliberated, Sarah arrived. Joey headed in his trainer's direction, and the two of them left for the round pen.

That's it! Follow the leader. Lauren moved several feet away from Speckles and pulled a clump of grass.

"Yum, yum! Oh, Speckles, this is delicious!" she exaggerated, pretending to eat the grass.

Brown ears pointed in her direction, then his head slightly cocked to the side. Lauren dropped the clump and ran to another spot, tapping on the ground.

"Speckles! Look at this clump. Wow!"

She felt ridiculous. And then he moved.

Speckles, eyes narrowed and assessing, took several steps toward her. He lowered his head where her finger had just been and ate the grass. Stunned for a moment that it had actually worked, Lauren just watched him eat before repeating the exercise. Again and again she pointed out grass, and again and again the hurting horse followed. She played until her own legs began to hurt, then she sat down in the field.

"We're quite a pair, aren't we, Speckles?"

The paddock gate opened, and Sarah led Joey back into the field. He cautiously approached his pasture-mate. Would he be accepted? Joey's nose bumped Speckles' ear. Lauren held her breath. Speckles didn't move. Thank goodness. Joey was allowed back in. Speckles' pain had diminished just enough that Joey could once again get close.

Lauren sighed in relief. Speckles began to relax.

But as Lauren gathered up the tack, she couldn't let go of a nagging question: How much longer until the next crisis?

The answer came sooner than anyone could have anticipated. Week after week, Speckles continued to decline. Eventually, any kind of training was out of the question.

"The best we can do is try to make him comfortable," Dr. Gallagher said after examining Speckles at the ranch one evening.

Kim, Lauren, Sarah, and Barb gathered around the vet.

"Speckles' various problems have escalated to the point where treating one will severely impact the others. His only real option now is pain management. I am sorry that I don't have better news."

Dr. Gallagher gave Kim two different medications for Speckles and left the four women to absorb the news. They stood in silence for several minutes.

Lauren felt as though she had been punched in the gut. Speckles had always had good days and bad days. Less than four months ago he had been doing so well—well enough to steal a side mirror. Lauren had just assumed his bad days would eventually end and her beloved speckled monster would once again emerge to wreak havoc on unsuspecting volunteers.

"Okay, girls," Kim said, breaking the silence. "Our job is to take care of our Speckles and keep him as comfortable as possible. He's part of the Hope Reins family, and so we do what we need to do, right?"

Her tone energized the dejected women—Lauren most of all. Kim grabbed her hand and then Sarah's. Each woman took the hand of the one standing next to her, and they prayed. For comfort and healing for Speckles, strength for them, and faith to endure whatever was to come.

Lauren went to the ranch often, just to be with Speckles. On days when his pain was tolerable, she went into the paddock. Joey would stand on one side of Speckles, often resting his head on Speckles' back, while Lauren stood on the other side—sometimes brushing him, sometimes stroking him, but always happy just to be with him.

Other days were heartbreaking. When it was clear his pain

was so intense that not even Joey could get close, Lauren would pull a chair up to the fence and sit and read to him. He would pace and whinny, his bloodshot eyes searching wildly for relief. All the while she would keep reading, forcing herself to maintain a steady rhythm, willing herself not to break down and cry.

It was so hard to watch him decline. So heartbreaking to see Joey try to console his friend only to be rejected with a nip or a half-hearted kick. Speckles would create an invisible perimeter around him when his pain was too bad. Joey, somehow figuring out where the perimeter was, would stand right on the line. Not too close, but never too far.

———— · ————

March 19 dawned bright and clear at Hope Reins. Clumps of daffodils seemed to dance in the morning breeze. Tulips, ready to burst forth in full bloom any day now, filled the mulched beds. An intoxicating scent—was it honeysuckle or jasmine?—floated in the air as Lauren walked past the Hope Reins garden.

The garden was designed to give the children something to care for and nurture while they were at the ranch. Lauren loved how Kim and her staff were always coming up with ways to help point hurting kids toward hope. What seemed like a simple garden could so easily become a springboard for a conversation about the importance of being firmly rooted, the patience of a gardener, or how growth takes time. *Yes, a garden was a great idea.*

Lauren reached paddock two and stopped for a moment. A familiar fear gripped her. *What will I find today?* Would Speckles let her come in? Or would his pain say *Keep your distance?*

How her heart broke for this horse, this broken horse who was helping her feel whole. This horse who was teaching her things about herself—teaching her how to deal with her own pain.

He was standing near a tall stump in the middle of the field with Joey guarding his flank several feet away. Lauren's heart dropped. *Another distance day.*

As she called a greeting, Speckles looked at her. Not with wild eyes, not with a warning, but with . . . what? Lauren leaned over the fence, straining to see. His eyes found hers. He looked at her with what she could only interpret as longing. Did he want her close by? *Only one way to find out.*

She released the latch on the gate and entered the paddock. Joey's head turned toward her, his ears following her movement. Speckles' eyes honed in on her, following her every step.

"Hey, bud." She spoke softly, reverently. "How are you today?"

She lifted her hand to stroke his neck, to express the love that filled her heart. He jerked away, fear in his eyes. He couldn't receive her touch.

She lowered her hand as her throat tightened up. *Lord,* she started to pray silently. No other words came. Should she leave him? Should she stay?

Joey made a low, mournful nickering sound. Speckles didn't move. Joey's head tilted to the side as if trying to decide if he could come any closer. He did not.

"Oh, Speckles," Lauren lamented. "What can I do for you?"

A sharp pain shot through her knee, causing it to jerk involuntarily. She steadied herself by putting her hand on the tree stump. *Not now, Lord. Please don't let my pain keep me from being here for Speckles.*

Whiskers tickled her hand. A brown-and-white muzzle pressed into her hand. Speckles was touching *her, breathing on her*! His black eyes searched her face, the light in them quickly fading. As if someone were closing a curtain. At once she knew. Deep in her heart, as if spoken directly to her soul, she knew what was happening. Somehow, someway she knew that this was good-bye.

But he was still young—only seven years old! He would recover, right? She choked back a sob. *I cannot lose it right now.* He needed her, and she would be there for him. It was the least she could do. It took every ounce of restraint, but she did not touch him. Instead she just stood there, talking softly to the horse whose chin rested on her hand.

"Oh, my speckled love," she whispered. "You have suffered so much on this earth, but soon you will suffer no more. Soon you will run free in a place of eternal beauty and goodness."

Lauren knew many people didn't believe that animals went to heaven, but the Bible specifically mentioned Jesus coming back to earth on a horse. The book of Revelation described lions and lambs lying down together, and so she chose to believe that heaven would be full of animals—animals free to live as God created them, free from the effects of sin.

Speckles' lips tickled her hand.

"Apples, carrots, hay! You will have an eternal supply of all your favorites."

His whiskers fluttered like butterfly kisses on her hand.

"You will be free. But I will miss you . . ."

Tears silently rolled down her cheeks. Speckles lifted his chin off her hand. The spell had been broken. Lauren straightened her back and rubbed her knee. Speckles slowly made his way to the hay box with Joey following from a respectable distance.

Lauren turned to look for Sarah. *She needs to know about Speckles.* Lauren just couldn't shake the feeling that he had been telling her good-bye.

The moment she saw Sarah, Lauren heard Speckles fall. His legs had buckled beneath him, driving him to the ground. As if surrendering to the pain, he lay on his side, not even trying to rise.

Lauren heard someone yell for help. It was her own voice. She ran to Speckles' side. His eyes, full of pain and trust, looked up at her. *His meds.* Her mind raced. *He needs his pain meds.*

"I'll be right back, Speckles. Right back," she repeated, heading toward the tack shed where oral syringes of his meds were kept.

"Joey," she said, "stay with him."

Joey lowered his head, sniffed Speckles, and bumped his side. He obediently stood vigil.

"Good boy, Joey," she called out as she hurried from the paddock, nearly colliding with Sarah.

"Speckles is down! I'm going to get his pain meds," Lauren explained, continuing to run.

The pain in her knee was all but forgotten as she grabbed the syringe, yelled for one of the volunteers to get the trailer ready for a transport to the vet, and raced back to Speckles. Sarah was on the ground with him.

"Okay, bud, let's get this medicine in you so we can get you to the vet," she said, holding the liquid-filled syringe up to his mouth.

He took it without a fight.

"I just gave him enough for a Clydesdale," Lauren said to Sarah, stepping away from Speckles. "Hopefully, it will take effect soon."

Lauren filled Sarah in on what had transpired before she arrived. Sarah closed her eyes. She kept shaking her head as if it were all too much. It was. The midmorning sun warmed Lauren's face as she waited for any sign that Speckles' pain was lessening. "We need to let Kim know." Lauren pulled out her phone and called.

"We'll get him there," she said, after Kim told her that she would call Dr. Gallagher. "Tell them we'll be there as soon as we can. And . . ." She hesitated before adding, "Tell them that he is in really bad shape." Her voice caught on the last few words.

Several minutes passed with no apparent change in Speckles' condition. But then a leg straightened and then another. He thrashed his head. Made one attempt to stand, and then another. Finally, he was up.

"Okay, Joey," Sarah called, clucking her tongue.

Joey stayed close to his pasture-mate. Speckles was less than steady, but at least he was standing.

"I forgot to tell the volunteers to hook the trailer to my truck," Lauren said.

Sarah nodded. "Speckles is okay for the moment. Let's go help get the trailer attached."

The two women jogged over to the parking lot to inform the other volunteers of the plan. Lauren was suddenly grateful that she had been having car trouble this morning, because she'd had to borrow her husband's truck—a vehicle large enough to handle the trailer.

The handful of volunteers hooked up the trailer quickly, and Lauren and Sarah returned to the paddock to get Speckles. They stopped short of the gate. Joey and Speckles stood facing each other, engaged in what almost looked like a dance.

Joey pranced forward while Speckles took several steps back. Then they reversed the roles. Their heads rubbed against each other, muzzles bumping and manes tangling. They pawed at the ground and let loose several loud neighs. They were . . . playing.

"How much of that stuff did you give Speckles again?" Sarah asked.

"Apparently enough," Lauren answered, her heart swelling with a mixture of joy and pain.

They look so happy and content. Lauren was the first to enter the field. She walked up to Speckles like she had so many times before and put a halter on him. She secured it around his head. Joey was no help whatsoever, nuzzling Speckles and pushing against Lauren's hand.

Joey positioned himself between Speckles and Lauren. Lauren tried to get around Joey, but the determined horse blocked her move. Sarah stepped through the gate and walked over to Joey.

"Hey, Joey," she called out, her voice sounding much lighter than Lauren knew she felt. "Bud, we've got to let Speckles go," she said, quickly adding, "to the doctor. We need to let him go to the doctor, okay?"

Sarah rubbed Joey's neck. She started to walk toward the middle of the field in hopes that Joey would follow. He did not. Sarah pulled a treat from her pocket, and Joey moved toward her, finally leaving Speckles' side. Lauren quickly led Speckles through the gate.

Sarah lingered a moment with Joey. Acutely aware that his pasture-mate was gone, Joey stomped the ground and let out a whinny. Speckles nickered back from outside the fence. Joey trotted to the gate and waited for Sarah to take him, too.

Waited for someone to remove the obstacle that was keeping him from Speckles.

Lauren tried to swallow the lump in her throat. *I have to get Speckles to the trailer.* She forced one foot in front of the other, each step releasing one more tear. Unable to move past Joey standing guard at the gate, Sarah shimmied through the fence rails. Lauren risked one last glance at Joey. A gut-wrenching cry from him nearly broke her heart.

She swallowed her own cry. *Oh, Joey. I am so sorry.*

Speckles loaded onto the trailer easily. Thankfully, between the large dose of painkillers and a handful of carrots, he had walked up the ramp as if it were a part of his daily routine. The women drove in silence to the clinic.

Kim's car was already in the parking lot when they arrived. She and Barb, along with several vet technicians, met Lauren and Sarah to off-load Speckles.

Lauren provided more details to Kim as they all followed Speckles to a stall where an IV was started. The four from Hope Reins watched him for a moment before going to a small waiting room.

Thirty minutes later Dr. Gallagher came in. His face was somber.

"Ladies, I am so sorry, but there is nothing more we can do for him," he said quietly.

Lauren grabbed Sarah's hand.

"His conditions have escalated to the point that they are more than his broken body can overcome. I believe we have no choice left but to let him go."

Lauren's mind fought against the words she was hearing.

"I know this is hard, but it's what is best for Speckles," she heard him say. The words sounded so far away, even though Dr. Gallagher was right next to her.

"But you are the ones who make the final decision. We can send him home with large doses of painkillers and anti-inflammatories. It won't cure him, but it will hopefully keep him comfortable during his last few days."

Kim looked at Barb, Sarah, and Lauren. "What do you think?"

No one answered. Sarah pulled at the neck of her shirt. Barb wiped her eyes with the back of her hand.

"We have to let him go," Lauren said, breaking the awful silence. Tears were streaming down her cheeks, and her face seemed on fire. "It's time."

"I agree," Kim said, grabbing Lauren's hand. "Sarah? Barb? We have to make this decision together."

"Yes," they both whispered.

Dr. Gallagher nodded. It was time to say good-bye.

I can't breathe, Sarah thought. *I need to leave and get some air.* But she couldn't leave Speckles—he was resting now, so calm and trusting. A flood of memories washed over her. Memories of being scared of the unusual-looking, biting, kicking horse. Memories of him charging Joey during feeding time, and of Lauren wagging her finger in his face, reprimanding him like a child, telling him to share.

She remembered the first time Speckles had approached her after they learned how much pain he was in. She had been scared that he was going to lash out at her, but instead, he had rested his head on her shoulder. She remembered the wonder on Kim's face as she told the team about Speckles' encounter with Nathan at the Christmas event—the little boy and the big horse blowing air on each other, connecting in their own special way. Now, without thinking, Sarah reached her hand across the stable door to touch his face.

The horse stepped toward her and pressed his forehead into her hand. She splayed her fingers on the white splotch between his eyes. She leaned into the horse, the horse who had shown her the importance of not making snap judgments, of looking deeper than what you first see.

She inhaled his scent, the scent that brought Joey such comfort. *Oh, Joey!* How would he survive without his dear friend? And why did this beautiful horse have to endure such pain in his short life? Sarah hid her face in Speckles' cheek, her tears wetting his muzzle. Lauren and Kim hugged her, and they all caressed Speckles.

"I . . . I can't stay," Sarah admitted.

Kim squeezed her shoulder. "It's okay. I think we should tell him our good-byes and then go."

Sarah felt both relieved and guilty. She stroked his distinctive face once more, then headed to the restroom, where she could cry with abandon.

Lauren couldn't bring herself to leave. Not yet. She just needed another minute with her boy.

"Oh, my speckled monster," she cried. "How am I ever going to get used to you not being here?"

He pressed his nose to hers, breathing on her chin. Lauren threw her arms around his neck and hugged him, something she hadn't been able to do for weeks. His neck curved around her as she wept. Wept for her loss and his. Wept for what should have been, and what would never be. She drew a steadying breath, and he backed away from the stall door.

He turned to the back of the stall where it opened out to a

small paddock, an area where the veterinary team assessed an animal's motion. Lauren watched in awe as Speckles, temporarily free from pain, began to run. He ran and ran, his mane and tail flying wildly. He even bucked and reared. He almost looked joyful.

She wanted to call him to her one last time, wanted to touch him one last time. But she knew from the look in his eyes that he wasn't aware of anything anymore, not even her. She didn't want to leave, but she knew it was time for her to go. Somehow, she and Joey had to face a world without their best friend.

"Good-bye, sweet boy," Lauren whispered.

A few minutes later, the four women stood together in the small waiting room, holding on to each other.

"Lord," Kim prayed aloud, "we need you. This is so hard. It's too hard to bear on our own. Fill us with your strength right now. Wrap your peace around us. God, thank you for Speckles—short as his life was. Thank you for allowing us to give him a second chance. God, we do not understand your ways, but we trust that you are good and that you will help us through this."

She squeezed Lauren's hand. "And please be with our sweet Lauren, who has been such a champion for Speckles. Hold her close, Lord, and be her strength. We ask this in your precious name, Jesus. Amen."

The four women gave up trying to fight their tears and grieved the life of a broken horse together.

Kim followed Lauren and Sarah back to the ranch. The three of them unhooked the trailer and cleaned it out, thoroughly washing away every last trace of Speckles. She couldn't believe that he was gone. Gone. Just like that. Kim slammed the door to the trailer and locked it.

She worried about Lauren. And Sarah—she was taking this extremely hard. Kim knew this loss was going to have significant effects on her team. But she feared Joey would take it the hardest.

Kim sent the three women home; it had been an exhausting afternoon. She texted Mike to let him know what had happened and that she would be late. He offered to come stay with her, but she needed a few minutes alone. Kim climbed up on a picnic table to sit, waiting for the evening feeders to arrive. She wanted to let them know about Speckles. When she got home, she planned to send out an e-mail to all of the volunteers and Hope Reins families.

Pain gnawed at her heart, starting to break through her numbness. Had she done enough for Speckles? Should she have taken him in to the vet sooner that first time? Was this her fault? She straightened her shoulders and took a deep breath. Now was not the time to fall apart; there was too much that needed to be done.

A whinny came from paddock two, where Joey was pacing along the fence line. He cried again, then paused—waiting for an answer that would never come. Kim walked over, knowing the only comfort she could offer him was her presence.

Joey ran to the gate the second he heard the hinges squeak. He lunged past Kim, desperate to greet his pasture-mate.

"He's not here, baby," Kim whispered. "But I am."

She reached out to touch his neck, but he jerked away from her.

Where is he? Joey's body language demanded. *What have you done with him?*

Kim stepped toward the horse. "Lord, show me how to help him," she prayed. Every inch of him was on high alert, listening for any indication of Speckles.

"I'm here," Kim repeated, placing a hand on Joey's back.

He stomped his front legs and released a whinny.

"You're not alone."

Kim laid her head on Joey's back, finally freeing her sobs.

"You're *never* alone."

CHAPTER 16

"WHAT ARE WE GOING TO DO?" Kim asked Lauren and Sarah. "Joey just stands in the field all day. The feeders tell me he's hardly eating any hay, and he isn't grazing. It's heartbreaking to watch."

It had been a week since they lost Speckles. Seven days of Joey's frantic, plaintive cries. Seven days of Joey pacing along the fence line.

The three women stood outside paddock two. Joey had finally stopped pacing, but now he was just there. His agitation had given way to complete disengagement. Everyone was becoming concerned.

"Maybe he needs a distraction," Sarah suggested. "Possibly take him out of his field for a training session."

The idea had merit. They had suspended any formal training sessions with Joey, thinking he needed time to adjust before placing any demands on him. But maybe it was time to get him back into a routine.

"I'll do it," Lauren offered, her voice sounding oddly flat, even to her own ears. "I'll take him over to the arena."

Lauren attempted to reassure Kim and Sarah with a smile, but the pain was so raw. She still felt disoriented, like her life was happening at a slower pace than the rest of the world. She would fall into bed exhausted, but night after night, sleep would elude her. She knew Rick was getting worried about her.

"Let it all out," he would say, encouraging her to talk. But she feared that if she let it all out, she could never rein it back in. She only allowed herself to cry when she was in the shower, the stream of hot water minimizing her constant headache, and the sound muffling her sobs from her girls.

How much longer do I have to endure this pain? A few friends who had never been able to understand her relationship with Speckles would remind her that Speckles was just a horse. As if that were somehow supposed to be helpful. They had no idea what they were talking about. Speckles was not *just* anything. He was a horse, yes, but he had been so much more. He had been her support system, her mirror, her . . . It was still hard to process all that he had been to her.

"We'll stay close by in case you need us," Kim said with concern.

After getting Joey's halter from the tack shed, Lauren entered *his* paddock, not *theirs*. It was still hard not to call out for the "boys." Would it ever feel normal to see Joey standing alone, without his counterpart close by? Probably not. She fastened the halter around his head and held the lead rope just under his chin, pulling slightly to get him to move. He wouldn't budge. Maybe he simply *couldn't*.

"Joey, would you like to get out of here for a little while?" she asked, flatly. "We can just take a little walk."

She gently pulled again. The horse had no interest in following her, and she suddenly realized that she didn't have the strength to keep trying. She was exhausted and everything hurt. Her outside hurt today just as much as her inside. Every joint was on fire, and a migraine was ramping up. Lauren took Joey's halter off, kissed his neck, and left him standing right where she had found him. Maybe he just needed more time.

What are we going to do with him? Kim lamented in her mind, watching the dejection in Lauren's body language. Her shoulders slumped as she exited the paddock. Kim worried about both the horse and her volunteer.

It was clear Joey was not in a good place. Kim knew that horses grieved, but she had never witnessed it up close like this before. Certainly never to this degree. She and her team had discussed putting a new pasture-mate in with him, but he just wasn't ready for that, and neither were any of their other horses.

Finding a new companion for Joey was going to be tricky. He was needy, and he was different. Would any of their other horses get that? Would they be able to understand him like Speckles had?

Lauren silently walked past Kim, averting her eyes. Joey let out a soft whinny. Kim felt like a weight was pressing down on her. How could she help these two? She felt so powerless. So clueless. So . . . blind.

Over the past few days, volunteers, staff, and even some of the children had expressed concerns about Joey. They were all depending on Kim to help him. But she had no idea how.

Lauren and Sarah approached Kim.

"I guess you saw how well that went," Lauren said.

"It's okay," Kim replied, trying to reassure her. "Let's give him another week or so. We'll figure this out."

———

Two weeks passed with no real change. Joey continued to stand in the middle of his field, not grazing, not walking—just standing. It was as if he wanted to disappear, as if he wanted the ground to swallow him up.

Sarah and Kim visited him every day, trying to coax him to eat, to drink, to engage in some way. Nothing came easily with him anymore. Tasks he used to do with ease—being led from his field, being groomed, walking around the arena—now seemed to take every ounce of energy he possessed. It was true for everyone caring for him too.

"Come on, big guy. You have to eat something," Sarah pleaded, waving a handful of hay under his nose. He took a few stalks, but even those were dropped.

"Oh, Joey, what do you need from us?" Sarah asked, wishing more than anything that this special horse could talk to her.

Instead, Joey turned around, facing away from Sarah. He had shut her out. She knew the posture well because she had used it herself on several occasions. Joey's ears continued to shift and rotate, always listening, always on alert for the sound he longed to hear more than any other.

"Sarah?" a young voice called out to her from outside the fence. Sarah recognized a little girl named Amy; she and Joey had met a little over a month ago during a session. "Can Joey play with me today?"

Amy's mother was talking with Barb. Sarah looked at Joey, who was still turned away, then walked over to the fence.

"I'm sorry, but Joey can't play today. He's just not feeling up to it."

"Why?" the girl asked, sadness furrowing her brow.

Sarah didn't know what to say, how much to say.

"Well . . ." She took a deep breath. "He . . ."

Barb quietly came up and wrapped her arm around Amy's shoulders.

"Hi, Amy. Are you ready to go get a horse?"

"I want Joey," Amy said, her bottom lip jutting out slightly.

Barb pulled the girl in close, whispered something in her ear, and led her toward Shiloh's paddock.

Sarah watched as Amy looked back at Joey. When would Joey be able to return to sessions? Would he ever be able to? He had already suffered so much loss in his life. Was this most recent loss going to be too much for him to endure?

Another question began tugging at her mind, one she couldn't allow herself to fully process: What if Joey can't be used in sessions anymore? What will happen to him? Will they still keep him? She instantly shook the thought away. Of course they would keep him. He was Joey. He was family, and they would see him through this.

A spark of urgency began to flame inside her. They had to help him through this. But how?

Sarah was in the tack shed taking inventory later that afternoon when Lauren walked by. She called out to her, but Lauren didn't hear. Or had she? It had been at least a week since Sarah had seen her at the ranch.

Lauren's extended absence had not gone unnoticed. Kim hadn't been able to reach the dedicated volunteer on the phone or by e-mail.

Sarah watched Lauren walk intently to Joey's paddock. Lauren's body language mirrored Joey's. Both of them held their heads low, both looked at the ground, both appeared so broken.

Why am I here? Lauren wondered, stepping into the paddock. What had possessed her to come? Surely this was the last place she needed to be. *I should leave.* The gate slammed closed behind her.

Joey looked so lost and incomplete. It was weird, but Lauren found herself jealous of Joey. How she longed to just stand and grieve. Cry for the horse she missed so much. Cry for herself and the never-ending pain that plagued her heart and body.

But she couldn't shut down. She had two daughters and a husband who needed her. She had responsibilities at home. She had to keep moving, keep working, keep going. Day after day she forced herself to complete each task, each chore, not allowing herself to think about Speckles. She had even asked for subs to fill in for her on the feeding team. There were so many reminders everywhere on the ranch, making it too hard to shove the pain down.

She needed to function, and so she stayed away for a week. She busied herself. She scrubbed every room in her house and threw herself into homeschooling. She trained her dogs and made plans for a garden. Her every waking hour was filled with business. But then night would fall. Night was awful. Dreams, images, and scenes flashed through her subconscious. She had no control over her thoughts. Her mind became a looping reel of memories, some painful, many beautiful, all resulting in a tearstained pillow. Rick held her night after night.

"You should go back," he would whisper in the darkness.

A part of her knew Rick was right, but how could she face

Joey again? She had all but abandoned him the week after Speckles died. Yet as each day passed, she felt a pull to go back. She wanted to see Joey again, to let him know that he hadn't lost her, too.

And so this afternoon after Rick had gotten home from work, she put on her muck boots, grabbed her keys, and headed to the ranch. Once she arrived, she walked from the parking lot to paddock two on autopilot. She thought she heard Sarah call out to her, but she couldn't stop. Couldn't talk. She had to keep moving forward, or she would turn around and run back.

She now stood beside Joey, the horse who had loved Speckles as much as she had, maybe even more. A gentle breeze played with her hair. She turned her face into it. The memory of Speckles with the side mirror hanging from his mouth suddenly came back. She was chasing after him, laughing as he proudly displayed his plunder to Joey. A single tear slipped from one eye. And then another.

Soon her tears fell in streams down her burning cheeks. A sob escaped her mouth. Her body shook as her carefully constructed emotional wall began to crumble. She hugged her stomach, pushing against the hollow pain that threatened to swallow her. Her mouth hung open, but now no sound emerged. Her silent cries shook her shoulders. *God, how long will this last?* She squeezed her eyes closed, trying to shut out the memories, the grief.

She nearly jumped when something bumped her shoulder. She spun around to see Joey's face inches from her own. *How long have you been there?* Lauren didn't move. *What are you doing?* She turned away from him, listening. She could hear him breathing. Could almost feel his whiskers on her neck. Joey lowered his head onto her shoulder. She felt the pressure of his lower jaw. The pressure grew in intensity. His head grew heavier and heavier, and his breathing slowed. Was he asleep? A long sigh escaped his nostrils, his air brushing against her neck. Something in her steadied, stilled, and her sobs subsided.

You need me. And I need you. She leaned her head back slightly. Joey sighed again, his head nuzzling into her neck. She would stand here as long as he wanted.

"I know, Joe-Joe," she whispered. "I know how much you miss him." She stroked his muzzle. "I miss him too."

Kim found Sarah leaning against the tack shed, her eyes riveted to something in the distance. She followed Sarah's gaze to Joey's field, where he and Lauren stood together. Together Kim and Sarah watched the tender scene—two broken souls finding comfort in each other. Kim knew they were observing something powerfully personal, private, and reverent.

Day after day Lauren and Joey would spend time grieving together. Lauren had thought she was going into Joey's paddock that first day to offer him some solace. It never occurred to her that he was going to help *her* begin to heal, that they would form their own support group.

During that initial bonding when Joey had laid his head on her shoulder and let out that long, shaky sigh, something had shifted inside her. Moments earlier, she had been standing alone in her grief, her thoughts, and her memories. Then, suddenly, Speckles' friend was standing with her. Understanding her in a way no one else possibly could. Joey got it, Joey felt it, and Joey was there. Lauren had gone into the paddock terrified of confronting her pain and had left knowing she didn't have to confront it alone.

Joey's consistent presence reminded her of someone else who had always stood with her. The person who knew her pain, who waited with arms open wide to help her bear it. She had been a Christian for a little while now. She knew Jesus loved her—was delighted by that love—believed that he had died to give her eternal life and risen to give her victory over sin, but she had never really understood the day-to-day relationship she could have with him. *What did that look like, feel like?* The closeness she could feel to a God she couldn't see. The assurance that she was never alone.

But the moment Joey pressed his head down on her shoulder, a verse had come to her mind. Jesus was praying for the crowds who had gathered to hear him, urging them to take his yoke upon them because it was easy to bear. Jesus promised "rest for their souls." *I need that, God.*

As she reflected, a soothing, calming warmth infused her heart. A few minutes later, her breathing had returned to normal and her tears had dried. The pain of loss was still present like a shawl hanging loosely across her shoulders. But it was no longer choking her. It was that awareness that compelled her to go to the ranch every following day.

Some days she spent hours with Joey, others just a few minutes. Sometimes she brought her daughters; other times she needed to come alone. By the second week, Joey would meet her at the gate, follow her to the back of the paddock, and graze. Lauren kept a hand on him at all times, a physical connection to something bigger and unseen.

After grazing for a while, Joey would nuzzle into her chest and then fall asleep—every single time she came. It was as if he had been exhausted from his grief, from his vigil for Speckles. Lauren helped carry his grief so he could rest. And in his rest—in their rest—Lauren prayed that they would one day begin to heal.

CHAPTER 17

"I THINK IT'S TIME," Kim said to Sarah, Lauren, and Barb one day in mid-April.

"Are you sure he's ready?" Barb asked.

Lauren answered with confidence. "He is."

"Well then," Sarah said, imitating a game show host, "let the search begin!"

Joey, although still a bit dejected and withdrawn, was at least acting well enough for the staff to begin introducing him to new potential pasture-mates. No one expected him to bond with another horse the way he had with Speckles, but Joey needed companionship. With his limitations, Joey depended on his pasture-mate for guidance.

But which of their horses was up for the job? Horses have personal space bubbles, and they communicate visually—the slightest tightening of a lip communicates volumes. Joey had no bubble, and he had a hard time sensing where other horses' bubbles were. Obviously, he could not read visual cues, which put him at risk. Other horses might see his differences as threats or misinterpret his limitations as confrontational or, worse, as a weakness. Yes, it was going to take a special horse with a unique temperament to share a paddock with Joey. There were ten possibilities.

Trying to lighten the mood after so many difficult weeks, Sarah suggested they treat the search like their own equine version of *The Bachelor*.

"We could have Joey give the winner a carrot instead of a rose," she joked.

The women chuckled, although all of them knew this was not reality TV. There would be real consequences if they put the wrong horse in with Joey. However, if they were ever going to figure it out, they had to get started.

Shiloh was the first choice. Her smaller size and mild temperament made her a favorite with the children. That was definitely something she and Joey had in common.

Since the two horses had been neighbors, sharing a fence for the past year, the team felt fairly confident that this could be a good match. After all, Shiloh had never taken issue with Joey in the past. Sarah led Shiloh into the new field, while Lauren held Joey on a lead rope. The plan was to introduce the two under close supervision so they could intervene if necessary. Joey's ears perked up at the sound of hooves. His head bobbed in anticipation, then stopped, listening and waiting.

Shiloh sniffed the air, then the ground, stomping in curiosity. Sarah allowed her to leisurely walk in Joey's direction. They would not force either one of the horses. This was just a trial visit.

The moment of reckoning finally came. Shiloh stepped within Joey's reach, and he stretched his head out. She sniffed, snorted—and nipped! Joey jerked his head back. Shiloh's lips were tight and her ears were back.

"It's okay, Shiloh," Sarah said soothingly. "Joey's your friend. Just give him a chance."

Shiloh seemed unimpressed with Sarah's pep talk. Joey approached her again. This time her teeth made contact. Joey reared back, turned away from Shiloh, and faced Lauren. That proved to be a mistake. Shiloh lunged forward, biting him on the rump.

"Girlfriend," Sarah said, navigating Shiloh away from Joey, "that is no way to earn a carrot from Joey!"

This match did not look promising. But after twenty minutes, Shiloh had not attempted to bite Joey again. Maybe there was hope after all. Sarah and Lauren unfastened the horses' halters and left the mare and gelding on their own while they went about their other tasks and duties within sight of paddock two. There was an occasional nip, an occasional whinny, but for the most part it seemed the occupants were getting along reasonably well.

Lauren left to pick up her girls when the evening volunteers began arriving. Sarah informed the team of the change in Shiloh's location and then watched closely as the others delivered hay to paddock two.

As Joey and Shiloh approached the hay box from different sides, Joey inadvertently moved his head into Shiloh's space. She reared up, bit, and whinnied. Joey stepped back, but Shiloh wasn't finished. She refused to let Joey anywhere near the hay box. Even after she was done eating, she continued to hound him and force him away.

The sight of sweet Shiloh bullying Joey was more than Sarah could handle. Joey had been through enough. Sarah moved Shiloh back into her original field. While the mare may have calmed down over time, Sarah wasn't willing to risk Joey's well-being on a maybe.

If Sarah hadn't known any better, she could have sworn that Joey was relieved when she led Shiloh out of the paddock. He was lonely, but obviously he wasn't *that* lonely!

"I agree, bud. No carrot for this one."

The next months brought a parade of candidates through Joey's paddock. Jesse and Essie, two other neighboring mares, were brought in one at a time. Neither lasted long, each reacting like Shiloh had. Gabe, the former party pony, also spent a short period of time with Joey, but the small gelding perceived Joey as a threat. Gabe repeatedly rammed his head into Joey and snapped his teeth in warning.

Joey was being a trouper about the disastrous pairings, but Kim and the others worried that the stress was taking a toll. Thankfully, Lauren continued to console him each day.

More time passed without a solution. Disheartened but willing to try one more mare, Kim and her team decided to bring in Abby, a beautiful Percheron.

The huge black draft horse had performed in dressage, the state fair, and the Special Olympics. But when the family who owned her were moving and could not take their beloved horse with them, Abby found a home at Hope Reins.

Kim considered the two-thousand-pound beauty a great asset, as sweet as she was big. Nothing seemed to rattle Abby, although her sheer size prevented her from moving as fast as the other horses.

Abby had eagerly followed Sarah from the large pasture to paddock two. She looked at Joey with curiosity. Joey seemed uninterested, and confirmed it by turning away from Abby and Sarah.

But then Abby let out an eager, excited nicker. Her large hoof, the size of a dinner plate, stomped. Joey made an about-face and pranced over to Abby. In fact, his knees were raised so high that he appeared to be strutting. Joey stopped to sniff the air. The mare was standing ten feet in front of him.

Sarah relaxed her hold on Abby's line, praying the huge horse wouldn't hurt Joey. She did have almost a thousand pounds on him. If Abby turned on Joey, it could get ugly. Joey took several more steps forward. Closer . . . closer. His nose bumped Abby's side. The black mare was momentarily startled but settled down quickly. She breathed in Joey's scent, sniffing his nose and his neck. Joey lifted his tail higher. He nickered and bowed his head toward her, bumping her chin with his. No biting, no rearing.

Sarah unfastened Abby's halter. Time for the real test to begin. *Please be good to him, Abby*, she silently pleaded.

The first day passed without incident. On the second day Joey's affection increased. He began nuzzling Abby, following her, and even nibbling along her back. Miraculously, Abby tolerated it all, including Joey's lack of respect for personal boundaries.

By day four, Kim, Sarah, and the whole Hope Reins team were feeling relieved. Abby seemed like a good match. Joey's attempts to show off for Abby with his exaggerated prancing and elevated tail were actually comical and endearing to everyone. Abby, while not overly impressed, was at least accommodating to her lovesick pasture-mate.

However, by the seventh day Joey's affections had turned into an obsession. He started becoming aggressive toward anyone who entered the paddock, afraid that they were there to take Abby away. He would still welcome visits from Lauren, but he would position himself between her and Abby. Joey would charge other volunteers entering the gate, stomping and crying his displeasure. By day ten, he had become so unpredictable and dependent on Abby that Kim decided the two horses had to be separated. Sarah escorted Abby out while four other volunteers tried to control a whinnying, rearing, angry Joey.

In the midst of the move, Sarah's phone buzzed with a reminder that sessions were starting in ten minutes. She hurried Abby, as much as Abby could be hurried, back to her field.

"He fell hard for you, didn't he? But look at you! You're gorgeous."

Abby's long black mane hung over her eyes, giving her a wild look.

"Joey will be okay," she assured Abby, as well as herself.

Once Abby was reunited with her pasture-mates, Sarah joined the other session leaders for a time of prayer before the families arrived. What had started as an obligatory going-through-the-motions routine before sessions had turned into a comforting occurrence for Sarah. Every day she found it a little easier to talk to God, whom she had ignored for so long. She still didn't understand why he had allowed her to suffer such betrayal in her life, but she was starting to believe that he hadn't completely forgotten about her.

Sarah had not planned on being at the sessions today until Barb mentioned that Aly was coming.

The girl had been back to Hope Reins a few more times since her first visit, but not since Speckles had died. Each time, she had worked with Joey—cleaning his paddock, leading him to the hitching post to be groomed, sitting in the saddle while Sarah led him around the arena. But she still had never uttered a word. As discouraging as it was, Sarah knew the time and effort were worth it, just for the way Aly looked at Joey with absolute love and trust.

Sarah's mind temporarily wandered as Kim prayed. *I need to tell Aly that she won't be able to work with Joey today.* He was too volatile right now—especially after losing Abby mere moments before. She could hear him crying and knew he was frantically pacing. *Oh, Joey.*

Sarah intercepted Aly and Cindy in the parking lot.

"Aly is looking forward to seeing Joey again," Cindy said, running her fingers through her daughter's thick curls. "She's been anxious to see him ever since you called us about Speckles."

Sarah remembered how difficult those phone calls had been. Kim had insisted that each session leader notify their Hope Reins families about Speckles' passing. When Sarah got in touch with Cindy and explained the situation, Sarah heard her repeat it back to Aly. A few moments later Cindy had said that Aly wanted to know if Joey was okay. Sarah had been blown away at the girl's insight and concern.

Now she knelt down to Aly's eye level.

"Oh, Aly, I am so sorry, but I don't think we will be able to work with Joey today. He's really sad and mad that his friend Abby had to leave his field. He's been kind of lonely without Speckles, and we tried to find him a new friend. But Abby isn't the right buddy for him, and Joey's pretty upset."

Sarah stood up to explain the situation to Cindy in more detail. The mother looked sympathetically at the pacing horse. Aly stood on her tiptoes and waved her mother toward her.

Cindy tucked her hair behind her ear and listened to Aly's whispered message, then smiled.

"Aly would like to know if she could just sit outside Joey's fence."

Sarah looked at Aly. *What a sweet little girl.*

"That is a great idea, Aly! I think Joey would really like that. He needs a trusted friend right now."

While Sarah led Aly over to paddock two, Jo Anne invited Cindy to sit and talk.

"Kiddo, we will need to stay back a little farther than usual today," Sarah said, wanting to be very cautious with the distraught horse. "Joey is really upset about Abby getting taken out, and I don't want him to accidentally do anything to hurt us."

Aly nodded, a look of understanding far beyond her years briefly crossing her face.

"Hi, Joey," Sarah called out. "I brought Aly over to see you. You want to say hi?"

The horse kept pacing, and his cries got louder. Aly put her hands over her ears. *Okay, maybe this was not such a great idea,* Sarah chastised herself.

And then Aly sat down several feet in front of Joey's fence, hands still covering her ears, eyes glued on Joey. Sarah sat down beside her.

The two sat in silence and watched the far-from-silent horse. Sarah clucked her tongue. No response. Joey continued expressing his displeasure.

Sarah looked at Aly out of the corner of her eye and saw her sitting stoically. She no longer had her hands over her ears; now she was twisting a blade of grass with her fingers. At least five minutes passed before Joey calmed down a little. He stood close to the gate, releasing long, exaggerated sighs.

Sarah motioned to Aly to stay where she was, while she approached Joey.

"Buddy, are you settling down?" Sarah asked, tentatively reaching out her hand.

Joey stomped the ground three times before sniffing her hand. Then he sniffed the air, clearly trying to detect where Abby was. With no results, he turned his head away from Sarah, yet made no effort to leave. Aly looked at Sarah, eyebrows raised in an unspoken question. Sarah nodded, inviting the little girl over.

As Aly came closer, Sarah whispered to Joey, "You be good to her. We need gentle Joey right now."

Aly looked so small standing near Joey, her head barely reaching his lowered chin. Sarah held her arm out, keeping the little girl at a safe distance. When Sarah clucked her tongue and reached her hand out again, Joey accepted a stroke on his muzzle.

"Aly, I'm going to get a treat for Joey. I want you to sit down right here and wait for me," Sarah instructed, pointing to a spot ten feet away from the fence.

The little girl followed Sarah's instructions. As Sarah was leaving, she passed a staff intern who had been hired right after the successful fund-raiser.

"Hilary, will you hang out with Aly for a few minutes? I'll be right back."

Sarah jogged to the feed shed and grabbed two alfalfa-and-apple horse cookies. But what she saw on her way back to the paddock slowed her down.

Aly's head was bobbing slightly, and her hands were moving. As Sarah caught a glimpse of Aly's profile, she noticed the little girl's mouth was moving! Was she *talking* to Joey? Sarah watched in wonder as Joey's head worked its way below the bottom fence rail and he began sniffing the ground in front of Aly. She was talking to Joey, and he seemed to be listening! *Oh, Joey, if you only knew the gift you've just been given! What is she saying to you?* Aly turned around. Sarah pretended to just notice her. She smiled and held out a horse cookie.

"I think Joey needs a special treat," she said. "What do you think?"

Aly nodded decisively.

Sarah walked up to Joey and clucked her tongue. He raised his head, honing in on the smell of his favorite cookie, and greedily took it from Sarah's hand. Sarah motioned Aly over and showed her how to hold the second treat. Aly bravely reached her hand through the middle slats. Joey lowered his large head and gingerly took the offered cookie. A radiant smile lit up Aly's face.

Sarah would have given anything to know what the little girl said to the horse. But honestly, what she said didn't matter nearly as much as the fact that she had said something. And, of course, it had been to Joey!

"We have to get a companion for Joey," Kim said several days later. "Which is why I've agreed to take Justin from the equine rescue league."

Not much was known about the reddish-brown quarter horse. He had shown up in the front yard of a woman's farm in Johnston County, south of Raleigh. After contacting the authorities, who tried to find the horse's owner without success, the rescue league began reaching out to local ranches. The volunteers there had named him Justin and described him as having a sweet, easygoing nature. He seemed a good fit for Hope Reins.

"With our current session schedule so full and the large group session with the Ronald McDonald House families coming up, I don't have time to make site visits," Kim explained to her team. "So we've decided to take Justin on a trial basis. If he works out, great. If not, he will be returned to the rescue league. Who knows? Maybe Justin's the one for Joey."

From the moment the medium-size gelding arrived, he and Joey got along. Justin accepted Joey, played with Joey, even attempted to guide Joey with gentle nips on the rear and head nudges. It seemed to be an instant connection—finally!

Four days later, Kim watched the two horses grazing together. After sending up a silent thank-you to God for providing such a great match for Joey, Kim started to head back to her office. That's when she saw Justin collapse—onto Joey! He just fell over, bumping into a very startled Joey before hitting the ground with a thud. Kim cried out for help as she went running into the pasture. But as she neared the fallen horse, his head jerked up, his legs straightened, and he stood up and began grazing, acting as though nothing unusual had happened.

"What in the world!" Kim exclaimed. Justin seemed absolutely fine, and Joey, who stood unmoving and alert, didn't seem to be hurt.

Several volunteers had come running, all of them looking puzzled. *Was it a stress reaction from the move?* The team gave the horses some room and tried to proceed as normal. But two days later, it happened again.

Kim called the rescue league, who sent a vet over to examine

Justin. After running some tests and observing a third collapse, the vet gave Kim the news: Justin suffered from narcolepsy.

"Narcolepsy!" Kim repeated, unable to keep from laughing.

Although it was rare, the vet explained, horses could suffer from a sleep disorder that caused such extreme drowsiness that the animal fell asleep instantaneously. Keeping a horse that could fall down without warning and possibly injure a child didn't seem the wisest idea. With his sleep attacks, Justin needed specialized care, more than Hope Reins could provide.

"Leave it to us to find a narcoleptic horse to guide our blind horse," Kim told her small staff and team of volunteers after the equine rescue league loaded Justin back onto their trailer. Justin had seemed like the perfect companion for Joey. Now that he was gone, they had to start the search all over.

Kim and her team sat at the round table in the Hope Reins office, facing a large whiteboard listing the names and temperaments of their four remaining horses. Pros and cons to each pairing were written down. They knew better than to put a strong-willed alpha male in with Joey, so that eliminated three of the larger geldings. And they had already tried all the mares.

They were down to one more option: Spirit. If the buckskin gelding didn't work out . . . well, Kim just couldn't even go there. Joey needed a pasture-mate; he was starting to show signs of withdrawing again. Lauren was working wonders with Joey, but he needed a horse companion.

Granted, the wheat-colored horse with a midnight-black mane had a stubborn streak, but he also tended to let things just roll off his back. Spirit had been a rodeo performer, which had taken a significant toll on his knees. After sustaining injury after injury, he was retired and eventually found his way to Hope Reins. After an initial period of adjustment,

Spirit had seemed to settle in well, although he still suffered from bad knee joints.

He appeared eager to please and happy around people, but when a weather front would move in, or after a long training session—those times when he was in pain—he would let everyone know that he was not happy. On those days, he would become aggressive at feeding time, intolerant of anyone coming into his paddock. He was also prone to kick when in pain. Spirit's limitations were similar to what Speckles had endured. *Maybe that's a good sign*, Kim dared to hope. Spirit was currently in his own paddock, but Kim took the marker and wrote Spirit's name next to Joey's on the whiteboard.

Kim arrived early at the ranch the next morning. She needed to spend a few quiet moments with Joey before Spirit was brought to the field. The impending introduction was weighing heavy on Kim. The what-ifs rapidly fired in her mind.

What if this doesn't work?

What if we can't find a pasture-mate for Joey?

What if I'm not doing enough?

She had more questions than answers because she couldn't see how it was all going to play out.

"Blind faith," she whispered. The phrase had been running through her mind a lot these days.

After greeting Joey with an apple and a rump scratch, she climbed into the hay box, just like she had done so many months ago.

"Joey-bear, you're going to meet a new horse today. His name is Spirit." Kim wound a piece of hay around her finger.

"He's a lot like Speckles. At least I hope he will be, in all the ways that matter."

Joey had finished his apple treat and cocked his head at Kim as if to say, *Oh, it's you in my hay box again.* "Oh, Joe," Kim said, touching his nose, "I know it's been hard without Speckles, and you have been through so much recently. But would you give Spirit a chance? We all need this to work out."

She handed Joey some hay. "We need you to come back to us. We miss you, Joey—sweet, goofy, gentle you. You think you can do that?"

Joey nickered, making Kim laugh. "Good boy."

Now if only Spirit would be so agreeable.

An hour later Spirit and Joey stood facing each other while Kim and a group of volunteers watched from outside the fence.

Neither horse made a move for several tense moments. Then without warning, Spirit reared up and whinnied. Kim knew it was a show of dominance. Joey whinnied back and bobbed his head up and down. Spirit whinnied louder. Then silence.

Would Spirit bite? Kick? Charge? Instead, he simply walked several feet away and began to graze. Joey made no effort to follow him.

"That's it?" Kim whispered, more to herself than her helpers.

The horses grazed for quite a while. Spirit made a few more dominance moves, but they were all for show—none were intended to hurt Joey.

Feeling it was far too soon to assume the best, Kim continued to watch the two horses day after day. The days turned into weeks, and the weeks turned into months with no incidents. Joey had a new pasture-mate. They fell into an easy rhythm. It was not a bond like that he'd shared with Speckles, but it was a companionship that seemed to ease his loneliness and grief.

Finally, Kim announced to her team at their weekly meeting that Spirit and Joey were official pasture-mates. "I'll take the winner's carrot to Spirit after the meeting," Sarah chuckled.

Everyone laughed, and the team released a collective sigh of relief.

"Well, I guess it's time to see if Joey's ready to get back into sessions," Kim said.

The laughter faded. No one said a word for several seconds, each person looking to another for comment. Each afraid of the answer, the possibility that losing Speckles had left Joey permanently changed—that he wouldn't be the same easygoing horse he had once been. Finally Lauren spoke up.

"He'll be ready."

CHAPTER 18

"Ow! Get off. Joey, move!" Lauren yelled from inside Joey's paddock.

It was the day after the staff meeting when she had confidently announced that Joey would soon be ready for sessions again. *What was I thinking?* At the moment, that question took a back seat to a far more pressing problem. En route to the open-air round pen for a training session, Lauren had almost made it to the gate when she had to sidestep a pile of manure. Joey, oblivious to the slight change in direction, kept walking, his hoof landing squarely on top of Lauren's boot. Her yelp had brought the horse to a complete stop.

"Get off my foot, Joe! GET OFF!" she screamed wildly.

Concerned about the hysterical human in front of him, Joey leaned forward, nudging her with his nose, his hoof still firmly planted.

"OWW!"

Lauren threw her arms around his neck and cried, begging him to move. Finally, she calmed down enough to release Joey's neck. The horse eventually took a step back, scraping his hoof along Lauren's brand-new boot, peeling back the leather and exposing her sock.

Joey munched on clover while Lauren gingerly removed her boot and sock. Her foot was red and throbbing, but she was able to move it around in a circle, flex it, and extend it. Other than being tremendously sore, the foot had survived being crushed by a nearly thousand-pound horse. The boot was a different story. She had recently splurged on these boots, the first new pair in years. A phrase floated through her mind: *That's why I can't have nice things.*

Carrying her destroyed boot in one hand and Joey's lead line in the other, Lauren hobbled out the gate. As she left Joey in the paddock, she mumbled, "You need to learn the command 'Back.' And I need to get another pair of boots, preferably the steel-toed kind."

After several days of staying off her foot, Lauren was ready to work with Joey again, with Sarah's assistance. Sarah served on the newly formed horse care and wellness team and had expressed interest in Joey's progress, knowing how much he connected with the children.

Getting Joey to cooperate with his new training schedule, though, was proving to be far more challenging than either Lauren or Sarah could have imagined. He had grown so used to Lauren's visits, when the two of them just spent time together and he would fall asleep. Now, waking him up and convincing him to follow her out of his field felt like a chore. But after

some carrot bribes and animated talking, the sleepyhead woke
up enough to comply.

The threesome arrived at the round pen, and Joey eagerly
went inside. But the moment he realized that Lauren had not
led him there for a casual walk, he started to pull against the
lead line, unsure of what was coming.

The past few days when Lauren was home, she had been
researching various training methods to use with blind horses.
The recent incident with Joey made it imperative to establish
an effective way to communicate with him. Lauren knew that
Joey was capable of so much more than they were asking of him.
He was an intelligent horse—she had seen that firsthand when
Joey had consoled her after Speckles died. Other trainers had
successfully taught vocal commands to blind horses. Joey didn't
need those commands to participate in sessions, but Lauren was
convinced he needed more mental stimulation.

She had discussed her thoughts with Kim and Sarah over
coffee the day before.

"I think you are right," Kim agreed. "We . . . actually I have
been so scared of him getting hurt that I've been hesitant to
push him too hard."

"I think we all have, Kim," Sarah clarified. "Joey was doing
so well, and he has been through so much, that we all just
wanted him to be happy."

Lauren took a sip of her chai tea. "I'm just hoping that when
Sarah and I work with him, teaching him and pushing him just
a little, it will help him thrive and adjust to Speckles' absence—
even more than bonding with Spirit has done."

Kim set her vanilla latte on the table and leaned forward.
"I don't know what I did to deserve you guys, but I am so

thankful for you and your insight." She looked at Lauren. "And as Joey's head trainer, go for it! See what he's capable of."

That night, Lauren joked to Rick that she planned to become like Annie Sullivan to Joey's Hellen Keller.

"Not a lofty goal at all," Rick replied, smiling.

The YouTube videos made it look so easy, Lauren thought. But unfortunately, the horse standing before her now in the round pen was acting very much like a frustrated Hellen Keller.

Just wave the lead rope back and forth in large sweeping motions, and the horse will back up. Well, apparently not this horse. Lauren gently swung the rope. Nothing. She swung it a little harder. Nothing. She swung it in large arcs back and forth. Without warning, Joey reared, his front hooves coming dangerously close to Lauren's head. She stopped and opened up some distance between her and Joey, so she could collect herself.

"He's just scared, and probably a bit aggravated," Sarah said. "But you're doing a great job."

Lauren gave a half-hearted laugh. "I don't know about that, but I'm not giving up on him. He'll get this. I just have to figure out how to teach him."

If only I could talk to Annie Sullivan, Lauren thought.

She clucked her tongue to get Joey's attention and asked him to follow her as she pulled forward slightly on his rope. He followed. After finishing a circuit around the pen, Lauren began gently swinging the lead rope again, commanding Joey to back up. She had seen firsthand with Speckles how a horse could be trained to move away from motion or pressure. Surely Joey had been taught all of this before, Lauren realized, thinking of his prestigious background. So why was he fighting it so much?

Actually, since Joey was defiantly resisting by standing like a statue, *fight* was probably not the right word.

"I don't get it," Lauren called out to Sarah. "He's rearing up one minute and freezing in place the next. What am I doing wrong?"

"Would you like a break? I can give it a try," Sarah said. Joey didn't respond positively to any of her attempts either.

Nearly an hour passed, and Sarah's patience began wearing thin. "This isn't working, Lauren."

Lauren took the lead rope from Sarah.

"Well, considering Joey's not trying to kick our heads off any longer, I'd say we're doing pretty well."

"True, but he doesn't seem to be getting it at all. I wonder if he ever will." A moment later she whispered, "Maybe he just can't."

When Lauren swung the lead line this time, she also tapped it with a flexible fiberglass training stick—a technique she had remembered watching in one of the many YouTube videos.

"Move back, Joey," she pleaded. "Just take *one* little step back." She increased the pressure of the tapping while continuing to swing the rope. "It's not that hard. Just step backward."

She stood nose to nose with the horse. "Move back! Just take one step . . ."

Joey's back leg moved.

Lauren stopped. She dropped her arm to her side, instantly ceasing all motion. She even stopped talking. Aware he had just done something right—something that caused the movements to stop—Joey twitched his ears forward. Lauren reached into her pocket and pulled out a carrot chunk. Her student scooped the treat off her hand with his top lip. Lauren raised her arm again and began swinging the line. Joey stood frozen, until Lauren began tapping the line with the training stick.

Joey stepped back, and his ears flew forward as once again Lauren lowered her arm. Joey stood alertly, as if awaiting further instructions. His determined trainer repeated the exercise again. This time, as soon as Joey moved his leg, she reinforced his response with "Joey, back," and a tasty reward. Joey moved back four times more before the training session was over. He had gotten it!

Lauren felt like she could do anything at that moment. As she began to lead him out of the round pen, Joey backed right into the wooden wall of the enclosure.

"Okay, you big show-off," Lauren said, laughing. "Let's save some of those skills for another day."

After they walked Joey back to his paddock, Lauren and Sarah couldn't help but giggle like little girls.

"He did it!" Sarah said excitedly.

Lauren smiled, too emotional for words. He *had* done it. *They* had done it. He had actually understood what she needed from him.

As she bent over to scratch the back of her knee, a sharp pain radiated up her back, creating a knot in her neck. *Ugh. Hopefully, future communication won't cause me as much pain!*

Lauren and Sarah watched Joey search for Spirit, stopping every few feet to listen for him. He finally honed in on Spirit's location near the adjoining pasture. Joey casually approached his companion, but didn't get too close. It made Lauren long for Speckles. How many times had she found the two Appaloosas standing side by side, their tails intertwined as they grazed?

Joey was certainly making progress, and things were indeed getting better, but loss was loss. No matter how much changed, someone very special would always be missing and greatly missed.

The next week, Sarah found herself training Joey solo. Lauren had called, saying she was in too much pain to work with Joey. Lauren had been doing so well for so long that Sarah had almost forgotten that she suffered from several different painful conditions. Her pain often went hidden behind a smile. Sarah knew that a smile could only hide so much, and sometimes a smile just wasn't enough.

Somewhat intimidated to train Joey on her own, Sarah had briefly entertained the idea of skipping a training day. But she knew Lauren would feel responsible for delaying Joey's progress, and Sarah couldn't let that happen.

Before heading to paddock two, Sarah had met with Kim to give her a progress report on the horse care and wellness team she was putting together. She had been recruiting volunteers to oversee one to three horses each, working directly with the trainers and vet to formulate and implement a care plan. Her position carried more responsibility and a lot more work than feeding and leading sessions did, but knowing she was helping care for the horses brought her a deep sense of fulfillment. Still, she feared that Kim or someone else would find out about her past, and that everyone would reject her if they knew who she really was.

And yet, she couldn't stay away. She needed to be at Hope Reins, for reasons she still didn't fully understand. And so every day she showed up, she could only pray that they wouldn't find out about her past. The irony of praying that her deception would not be revealed was not lost on her.

Sarah reviewed the list of commands she and Lauren had created for Joey to learn—useful things for him to know, such as walking forward, lunging, and lifting a foot. The list was ambitious, but Lauren believed the blind horse could achieve each and every goal.

"Joey's only limited by the limits we place on him." The comment Lauren made a few days ago had stayed with Sarah.

It was true. True for Joey, true for the kids they worked with, and maybe even true for her.

She shook her head to clear her mind. This was not the time for an emotional excavation. She had a job to do. Sarah decided to start with the easiest command: "Walk." Since Joey already followed them on a lead line, Sarah hoped assigning a word to the action would be picked up intuitively by Joey. She took Joey to the round pen, following the same route as always. Once she directed Joey to the middle of the circular enclosure, he proceeded to back up. Sarah chuckled, admiring his memory recall.

"Way to go, Joey, but today we're going to move forward instead of backward."

Holding the lead line knot just under his freckled chin, Sarah gave Joey the signal with her tongue and tugged slightly as she moved forward. Like a star pupil, he instantly followed. The moment his hooves left the ground, Sarah said, "Walk." Joey's ears flicked, but she knew better than to think he understood what she meant.

As she led him around the enclosure, she repeated the word over and over again. Was it working? Was Joey getting it? *Maybe I should stop and start over. Maybe I should teach him "Let's go" to signal it's time to walk and then say "Walk" when he is actually doing so.* Deciding to regroup, Sarah closed her eyes and stopped walking. Joey kept going. Since Sarah was holding the lead line loosely, Joey pulled it free as he passed by.

"Wait!" she called. "Joey, stop."

Ugh. He didn't know that command. Sarah retrieved the lead line, pulled back, and eventually brought Joey to a stop.

"Okay, Joey, that wasn't the best start. Totally my fault," she admitted. "Let's try again. And this time, let's begin with 'Stop.'"

For the next thirty minutes, school was in session. At first, Joey wasn't too happy when Sarah held the fiberglass training stick against his chest to signal him to stop. He lifted his front hooves off the ground in protest, startling her.

Sarah mulled over the situation. Surely, back in his competitive years, Joey would have trained for hours and been taught many commands. But everything must seem different without the benefit of sight. She clucked her tongue and pulled slightly on his lead rope to get him to walk again. After he advanced several steps, she placed the training stick against his chest and said, "Whoa." He kicked against the pressure and let out an intimidating whinny.

"Joey, I just want you to stop," Sarah lamented. "You know how to do this. I know you do." Sarah tamped down her frustration. Training him to stop in the normal way just wasn't working. She needed a new approach. One that signaled to him that it was time to stop, but wasn't jarring to him. She rolled her neck to release a kink, then began again. This time after signaling for him to walk, Sarah started slowing her pace in anticipation of stopping. She then applied gentle, but building, pressure against Joey's lead line while counting, "One, two, three." After "three," she said, "Whoa" and halted. Joey did too.

She repeated the exercise several more times. Eventually Joey connected the dots between slowing, pressure, counting, and stopping. Feeling emboldened by his progress, Sarah added "Let's go" and "Walk" to his vocabulary, pronouncing each word clearly and loudly. Knowing he would need several more training sessions to cement the commands but curious to see how much he had retained, she attempted to put all of his skills together.

"Joey, back," she directed the horse.

He tilted his head and chewed in concentration.

"Joey, back," she repeated, pushing slightly against his chest.

The horse took a step back.

"Okay, Joey, let's go," she commanded.

He moved.

"Joey, walk," she added quickly, as the horse walked around the round pen.

"Joey, one, two, three, whoa."

Joey had stopped on "three"!

"You did it, Joey! You did it," she cheered.

She scratched his back and patted his rear before leading him along the well-traveled route back to his paddock. She couldn't wait to tell Lauren that he had learned three more commands.

Four weeks later, as a breeze gave temporary relief from the late July heat, Lauren sat on Joey's back in the middle of the rectangular riding arena. *Am I crazy for riding a blind horse untethered from a lead line?* Maybe the new medication she had recently started was affecting her in more ways than intended.

Last night, this all seemed like such a great idea. Last night while lying in bed and listening to the gentle snores of her husband, the thought of riding Joey seemed inspired—a way to challenge the intelligent horse as well as help him connect even more deeply with hurting children.

But this morning, sitting in a saddle, the idea just seemed downright ridiculous. Still, she was committed. Or maybe she should *be* committed. Too late now. She had climbed on Joey's back and was determined to see what he could do.

He had learned so many commands in such a short amount of time. He had learned that "easy" meant to slow down, while "get up there" meant to speed up. He had figured out that "it's good" meant the way was clear with no obstacles. Joey had even learned that "easy up" meant he was facing a slight incline and needed to lift his hooves and head a little higher, while "easy down" implied the opposite. But Lauren's favorite commands were "Foot" (when she needed him to give her his hoof), "Come here, bud" (when she wanted him to move his head close to hers for a kiss), and "I gotcha" (to let him know that he was not alone in his fear). It truly was remarkable what he had learned.

As Lauren had watched him in a session the previous week, she started to wonder if maybe Joey's blindness had been God's gift to Hope Reins. She had seen a different side to Joey during their intensive training sessions. She had seen a glimpse of "show Joey" and "performance Joey." It was obvious that he must have been a strong-willed horse in his early days. He would have had to be. The schedule, the demands of that life, would have required such a temperament. That and his intelligence were great qualities, but most likely qualities that would have made him more horse than a therapy ranch could have handled.

To Lauren's surprise, she found herself thanking God for Joey's blindness. Not that God would have caused his blindness, but he certainly had turned something bad into something extremely good. It reminded her of the story of Joseph in the

Bible—his brothers sold him into slavery, and soon after that he was falsely accused of a crime and thrown in jail. But God did not abandon Joseph and eventually used all the negatives in Joseph's life for his good purposes.

That night the week before as she walked to her car, it occurred to her for the first time that Joey was a nickname for Joseph! *How fitting!*

Now it was time to put her trust in Joey and for him to put his trust in her.

Lauren was determined not to let him down.

"You sure?" Sarah asked one last time.

"As sure as I can be. Unhook him."

And just like that, Joey was freed from the lead line. As if knowing his security line was gone, he froze. Lauren did too. Then she inhaled deeply and exhaled loudly, trying to mimic a horse. *If I sound like a relaxed horse, maybe Joey will relax.*

"Okay, Joey, you've got this," she said. Taking the reins loosely in her hands, she said clearly and confidently, "Joey, walk."

And he did—taking exactly four steps. Then he froze.

Lauren squeezed her legs against Joey's sides. "Joey, walk."

The horse's head nodded, and his ears twitched. He wanted to comply and yet didn't—couldn't.

Sarah rubbed his chin. "Come on, bud. I gotcha; you can do this. Walk."

She took several steps forward, hoping Joey would follow. He did not. Sarah clucked her tongue and clapped her hands. Joey stepped toward her. She repeated the actions while taking several more steps, Joey slowly following behind. Lauren patted him on the shoulder. It was not the ride she had anticipated, but she was still upright and he was moving. When Sarah stopped clapping and clucking, Joey stopped.

"I got it!" Sarah suddenly shouted, pulling her phone from her back pocket.

What is she doing? It hardly seemed like the right time to post something to Instagram! But then Lauren heard a steady beat—a clicking sound—from Sarah's phone. *Of course! The metronome.* Everyone at Hope Reins had heard about Hank using a metronome app to let Joey know where Hank was while he made repairs in Joey's paddock.

Lauren winked at Sarah. "Great idea!"

Sarah tucked her phone back in her pocket and called out, "Joey, walk." And just like that, Joey followed the sound. Sarah led Joey around the arena twice, his nose occasionally bumping her back pocket. As they approached the gate the second time, Sarah turned the phone volume down as Lauren called out, "Joey, one, two, three, stop."

He stopped on "three."

"You did it, Joey!" both women exclaimed.

Joey tilted his head as if to say, *What's all the fuss about?* His look was rewarded with rump scratches and neck kisses.

Sarah and Lauren repeated Joey's riding lessons each day for the next week. And each day he grew more and more confident. By day four, Lauren was riding bareback. By day seven, Joey no longer needed the metronome. He responded to Lauren's vocal commands and adjustments to the reins. Of course, that first time without the aid of the app wasn't perfect. There were some missteps—her leg scraped against the fence a time or two, and Joey sped up when he should have slowed down—but he had done it. *They* had done it. That day—her first completely solo ride with Joey—with the sun beating down on her back, and with sweat dampening Joey's coat, Lauren brought him to a halt, beaming when he stopped on "two."

She had just ridden a blind horse around the large arena! A woman who had suffered for years from unseen, unknown ailments had just ridden a horse who couldn't see the ground below him. It was too much to take in at the moment. Besides, Joey needed to be congratulated and fussed over. But she would process this experience for months to come.

The exercise affected Lauren deeply, for she was just beginning to see a glimpse of how God had been leading her all these years—all these pain-filled years. He had never abandoned her but had always been right there.

She climbed off Joey's back and wrapped both arms around the horse. "Thank you," she whispered.

CHAPTER 19

THE SIGHTS AND SOUNDS OF autumn were evident throughout the ranch. Decorative apple crates, pumpkins, and scarecrows lent a festive feel to the horse farm. The trees lining the riding trail were arrayed in splendid colors, reflecting the artistry of their creator. Seasons came and seasons went, yet God remained the same—that was the foundation of Hope Reins.

However, the change in seasons brought shorter days and colder weather, and with no electricity at the ranch, sessions were coming to an end until spring of the following year.

I can't miss Aly's last session, Sarah thought. After leaving work, she grabbed a quick dinner at a McDonald's drive-through, then headed straight for the ranch.

The team of volunteers dispersed after the pre-session prayer, greeting the children as they arrived. Sarah spotted Aly and her mother and headed their way.

"Hey, Aly," Sarah said, giving her a hug.

She was delighted when Aly reciprocated with a soft hug.

Sarah hugged Cindy and said, "I can't believe this will be our last session for a while."

"I know. Aly is bummed about that. But I told her maybe we could come visit Joey on Saturdays during barn chores. You'll still be doing those throughout the winter, won't you?"

"We sure will. What a great idea. I think Joey would like that very much."

A wisp of a smile brightened Aly's face. A hug *and* a smile today! Now, if only the sweet girl would say something. As Cindy left to find a quiet place to work, Sarah could almost feel her discouragement. Aly had been coming to the ranch off and on for a year, and while she had made a lot of progress relating to her peers and to horses, it was obvious that Cindy was beginning to feel that her daughter would forever be trapped in a world of silence.

Sarah longed to impart some words of encouragement to Cindy. But what could she say? Sarah began to wonder if maybe she was being naive. She had no idea what Aly had endured before being adopted. Maybe just like Joey, who had suffered permanent injuries from being abused, Aly had suffered permanent injury from her past. Sarah felt defeat beginning to well up in her own heart.

Sarah and Aly headed to the tack shed. Sarah asked Aly to pick out Joey's halter. As they walked to paddock two, Sarah noticed Aly smile at Spirit, whom she had met during her last session. The little girl seemed happy that Joey had a new friend.

"All right, kiddo, let's go get Joey."

Aly's eyes sparkled as she approached her favorite horse with confidence. She held her tiny hand under Joey's nose, and his muzzle engulfed it as he inhaled her sweet scent. Aly wasn't afraid at all when Joey stepped closer.

"Joey's happy you're here," Sarah said on behalf of the horse. "Do you think he would like to walk with us to the hitching post?"

Aly nodded vigorously. She was too small to put Joey's halter on, so Sarah took care of that, then handed the lead rope to her. Her wide eyes gave away her excitement at the new responsibility.

"We need to lead Joey along the same path he always takes to his hitching post," Sarah instructed as they exited through the gate. "Since Joey can't see, we need to help him know where he is and where he's going. Going the same way to his post and the arena is one way we can help him feel safe."

Aly nodded and then purposefully took charge. At the hitching post, Aly and Sarah wound Joey's rope around the wooden rail.

Sarah handed her young partner a medium bristle brush to give Joey a quick cleanup, while Sarah inspected Joey's hooves. When they finished, Sarah said, "Would you like to ride Joey now?"

Aly ran her small fingers, the nails dotted with peeling red polish, along the spots she could reach on Joey's side and eagerly nodded.

"Would you like to try riding Joey bareback, without a saddle?"

Aly's eyes grew wider than Sarah had ever seen them. Her little lips parted as she looked lovingly at Joey. The first time Sarah had watched Lauren ride Joey bareback, she immediately thought of Aly. Sarah had loved riding bareback as a child. The closeness of your body to the horse makes you feel as if the two of you are one. She suspected Aly would be thrilled to have that experience.

After leading Joey over to the arena, she placed a thin suede bareback pad on him—so that his back wouldn't get sore—and secured the girth. Sarah helped Aly with her riding helmet and then gave her a boost onto Joey's back.

"Okay, sweetie," Sarah said, holding onto Aly's leg. "This is quite different from riding with a saddle, but it's a lot of fun."

Aly wound her fingers through Joey's mane as Sarah talked.

"Joey is very used to being ridden like this, so it isn't strange to him. And since I'm going to lead him with his halter and lead line, you just put your hands on either side of his neck and hold on." Sarah positioned Aly's hands on Joey's neck. "We won't even worry about reins today. You just enjoy your ride on Joey. But if you feel like you're sliding off when Joey starts to walk, push your bottom down more firmly, okay?"

Aly took in every word intently.

"I'm going to lead him very slowly at first so you can get used to it, and if you feel comfortable, we can pick up the pace a little. If not, we'll stop. Joey's ready. Are you ready, Miss Aly?"

A definite yes.

Sarah paused. *She reminds me of myself at that age.* She studied the now six-year-old. Aly didn't look like Sarah at all, and her background was totally different. And yet, for some reason, Sarah identified with the girl.

With Joey's lead line in her hand and Aly's trusting face looking down at her, Sarah felt her stomach tighten a little. *If only I could hear your voice.* Her thoughts were interrupted by Joey's impatient pawing at the ground. *Let's get moving here.*

Shaking off the feeling, Sarah clucked her tongue. "Joey, walk."

The horse immediately responded. Sarah glanced up at Aly, whose dimples expressed her obvious delight.

After they completed one lap, Aly's smile grew even wider. Just then, Heather, another session leader, entered the arena with Gabe and a young boy. *Oh no*, Sarah moaned silently. *Will we have to cut the session short?* She couldn't risk Joey getting distracted by Gabe.

She tried to get Heather's attention, but Heather's back was turned as she helped the boy onto Gabe's back. Sarah quickly decided the best plan was to let Aly ride Joey back to the hitching post, where they would end their session by grooming him again.

As she started to turn the horse back toward the entrance, a strange feeling came over her that made her stop. Somewhere deep inside her heart, she heard a clear directive to stay in the arena. Tears welled up in her eyes as she obeyed and resumed another circuit with Joey.

Heather smiled at Sarah as she led Joey in a wide berth around Gabe, nodding in silent understanding of the situation. "We'll stay over here," Heather called out. Sarah waved her thanks.

Let go.

Another inner command, this one seeming to come from inside her ear. *Let go of what?* She looked at the rope in her hand. The lead line? Why would she let go of that? If she did, Aly would be riding on her own!

God, is that you? Sarah gasped in silent wonder, overwhelmed at the thought that God would talk to her. The idea seemed crazy. The child had never spoken a word to Sarah. If she rode Joey without Sarah's guidance, she would have to talk—loudly.

The inner prompting was too strong to ignore.

"Hey, Aly, my friend Lauren has been riding Joey without a lead rope. We've been teaching Joey lots of new words, so many that he can walk without being led."

Aly looked at her expectantly.

"Would you like to try? You are perfectly safe on his back. Joey won't fall, but—" Sarah paused and looked intently into Aly's eyes—"he won't move if he can't hear you. We've trained Joey to obey voice commands, which means he has to hear his rider speak."

Aly blinked, but there was no other telltale expression on her face.

"If I loop Joey's lead rope around his neck, I can tie it off on his halter and make reins for you to hold. But he will have to hear you say 'Walk' for him to walk. He will need to hear you so that he feels safe. He'll be scared if he can't hear you."

Will she do it?

Can she do it?

"Aly, I know you can do this. But you have to decide, okay? Today is the last day you'll get to ride Joey for a long time. I can keep leading him if you want, or . . ."

Sarah was afraid to look at Aly, afraid she would see the girl shaking, not nodding, her head. Afraid that the strong impressions she had heard hadn't been from God at all, but merely her own wishful projections. After what felt like an eternity, Sarah looked at Aly.

She sat perfectly still, her back as straight as the hitching post, her pink lips pressed together in a line, her small hands clamped tightly to Joey's neck. She stared at Sarah without blinking, her brow furrowed.

Aly turned her head slowly to watch the other rider in the pen, who was riding Gabe on his own while Heather stood off to the side. Sarah could see the longing in Aly's eyes. She knew the little girl wanted to ride. *Please, God,* Sarah pleaded desperately from her heart.

Aly turned back to face Sarah, her eyes averted, her posture now defeated. Sarah clucked. "Joey, walk."

Stay. Once again, Sarah heard the order from the unknown source.

"Do you want to stay and try to do it on your own?" Sarah asked Aly.

An affirmative nod was the only reply she received.

Sarah shrugged. The little girl clearly wanted to stay in the arena. Sarah led Joey to the south side of the enclosure, offered up another silent prayer, and looped Joey's lead rope around his spotted neck.

"Okay, Aly, Joey's all yours. But he is going to have to know you are with him. He won't move unless you say, 'Joey, walk.' Take a deep breath, fill your lungs with air, and speak loudly to him. He knows I'm not holding on to him anymore, and he is a little nervous standing here without any connection to me."

Sarah saw a glimpse of fear cross Aly's face.

"You know how to lead him—lean in the direction you want him to go. He knows this arena well. It's just like when I was leading him. The only difference is that he needs to hear you, needs to know he's not alone. Think you can do it?" She paused before remembering to add, "You will say 'Walk' to get him to walk and then 'One, two, three, whoa' when you want him to stop. Ready?"

Sarah was a bundle of nerves. Her insides were churning, her McDonald's cheeseburger suddenly not sitting well. Aly was like a tiny figurine on Joey. She gave no hint she was prepared to move, made no attempt to open her mouth. Sarah waited and leaned in slightly, willing herself to hear something, anything. All she heard were Gabe's hoofbeats and his rider chattering.

She smiled at Aly, whose eyes were fixed straight ahead, her pink boots dangling on either side of Joey. A war was clearly raging inside the little girl. A fight for freedom from fear.

"Joey, walk."

It was a whisper of sound. Not loud enough to have been heard over a steady rain, and yet, it had been loud enough to break into Sarah's thoughts. *Aly spoke!*

Sarah stood motionless, watching Joey for any sign of movement. Nothing. The soft command hadn't registered with the big horse.

"Great job, Aly," Sarah said, forcing herself to remain calm, even though she wanted to jump up and hug Aly. "That was awesome, and I am so proud of you. Do you think you can do it again, but just a little louder? Joey didn't hear you because it's so noisy out here. We have to really speak up, so he can hear us."

Aly nodded, but then quickly looked away from Sarah. She kept a tight grip on the makeshift reins. The horse shifted slightly, digging at the ground with a hoof. This was new to him, and he was getting anxious.

How long should I allow this to go on? Am I doing the right thing? Come on, Aly. You can do it. Speak up. Just two words. Come on! You can . . .

"Joey, walk."

Joey's ears flicked back, indicating that he had heard the gently uttered words. But he was unsure of the source and who they were intended for. Sarah smiled at the girl's courage, forcing her hands into her pockets, trying to contain her excitement and focus on helping Aly speak just a little louder to Joey.

"Way to go, Aly!" Sarah encouraged. "He heard you that

time, but he is still a little too scared to move. He needs to know that you want *him* to walk. Can you say it just a little bit louder? For Joey?"

Sarah momentarily held her breath.

"Joey, walk!"

It was a clear, forceful command, made by a young, sweet voice.

As if he had been waiting for that command as much as Sarah, Joey began to walk. He held his head regally as if he, too, was proud of Aly. Sarah giggled when she detected a slight prance to his steps. Aly looked just as proud as the blind horse, her eyes shimmering with joy and confidence.

Aly leaned slightly to the right, and Joey responded. The horse knew this arena so well that he didn't really need directions, but Aly was taking her job very seriously. *Joey wants her to succeed too!* Sarah marveled. Aly's mouth was moving; she was talking to Joey, not just giving him commands! With just two words, everything had changed. A little girl's voice was unlocked. Aly had faced the fears that had held her captive for years. She had used her voice, not for herself, but for Joey.

Sarah was so wrapped up in the magical moment that she failed to notice a woman weeping at the entrance of the arena. Cindy had arrived in time to see Aly riding bareback, an amazing accomplishment. But then, unexpectedly, she had witnessed something monumental that shook her to her core with joy. Cindy's hand covered her mouth and tears streamed down her cheeks. Sarah didn't notice her, not yet. She was transfixed, basking in this sacred moment in which the little girl with no voice spoke up for the horse with no eyes.

CHAPTER 20

SARAH WAVED GOOD-BYE to Aly and Cindy as they drove down the gravel drive. The ranch had emptied quickly tonight. Still, Sarah lingered. So much had transpired with Aly, and it was affecting her deeply.

"Hey, girl," Kim greeted her as she headed to her car. "Everything okay?"

"Oh, hey, yeah, I'm good. Just processing the session I just finished with Aly and Joey."

Sarah forced a smile.

Kim studied Sarah for a moment. "Hang on a second. Let me just throw this stuff in my car, and we can talk."

Great. Now look what I've done. The last thing she wanted was for Kim to see her unmasked and . . . vulnerable.

"Tell me about the session." Kim was always interested in the children's progress as well as how the horses facilitated them.

Relieved to be talking about Aly instead of herself, Sarah recounted every moment leading up to the girl's courageous breakthrough.

"Are you kidding?" Kim squealed. "She talked? Sarah, that's huge!"

Kim hugged Sarah tightly. It was such a spontaneous, caring reaction that it shattered Sarah's emotional walls. Her bottom lip began to tremble, and a quiet sob escaped her. Then the tears began to fall uncontrollably.

"Oh, honey, what is it? What's wrong?" Kim asked with concern, tightening her hold.

It took Sarah several minutes to find her voice, and when she did, it was a hiccuping whisper.

"It's just . . . I haven't . . . Aly speaking . . . I need to . . ." She buried her face in Kim's shoulder and released the emotions that she had been hiding up till now.

But a moment later, Sarah pulled herself together and straightened up. "I'm so sorry, Kim."

Kim waved her words away. "No apologies. You are hurting, and I am here for you. Is there anything I can do to help?"

Sarah cleared her throat. "Watching Aly find the courage to speak tonight made me realize how scared I've been to speak up since I've been here."

The compassion in Kim's eyes compelled Sarah to keep going.

"Seeing how much she trusted Joey, how she chose to be brave for him, made me wish that . . . I don't know . . . that maybe I could be brave and trust someone too."

Without thinking, the two women had walked silently toward paddock two. They stopped at the fence, leaning on the top rail.

Kim quietly broke the silence.

"What would you want to tell that person whom you want to trust?" she gently probed.

Sarah gazed at Joey. *You've taught me more about trust than any human ever has.*

Then she whispered to Kim, "I would want to tell that person that I'm not who I pretend to be."

Sarah lowered her head. *If only the ground would open up and swallow me right now.*

"And who are you really?"

Sarah couldn't do it. She couldn't risk it.

An image of Aly riding Joey—speaking up for Joey so he wouldn't be afraid—flashed through her mind.

"I'm someone who was broken by deception as a child, and I have survived behind a wall of lies. It has hurt those I've cared about, but it has hurt me much more deeply."

Kim winced at her words, lightly resting her hand on Sarah's shoulder as she continued.

"I'm not even sure I'm a real Christian. I mean, I believe in God—I asked Jesus to forgive me for my sins when I was a kid—but when my mother and I found out that my dad had lived a secret life, I just got so mad at him. Nothing really mattered anymore, and I started doing some really wrong things."

She risked a glance at Kim. "I actually moved to Raleigh for a fresh start . . . after my divorce, after my life crashed and burned. Great role model, right? I'm pretty much damaged goods at this point—too far gone for God to forgive me."

"Sarah, what a burden you have been carrying all this time," Kim said, her eyes filled with tears. "I'm so glad you finally were brave enough to share it, and I'm honored that you felt safe enough to talk with me."

Nothing was said for several minutes as Sarah fought to regain control of her emotions. Finally, Kim posed a question. "Sarah, what do you see when you look at Joey?"

Sarah, confused by the abrupt change in subject, ran the back of her hand across her nose before answering.

"Um," she started, searching for the right description, "I see a beautiful and brave horse who touches people's lives every day."

"So you don't see him as damaged, disabled, or broken?"

"No, of course not."

"If you don't see Joey that way, why would you think that God sees you as anything other than his beautiful, brave child who touches people's lives every day?"

Sarah's throat constricted, then without thinking, she clucked her tongue to call Joey over. She suddenly needed to touch him.

"You really think God feels that way about *me*?" she whispered.

"I know he does," Kim replied firmly. "Sarah, all of us are works in progress. We all bring hurts and sins and brokenness to the ranch. But that's the beautiful thing! God takes our messes—our heaps of ashes—and turns them into something more beautiful than we could ever imagine."

Sarah was reticent to ask the next question.

"So I don't have to leave? I can keep serving at Hope Reins?"

"What? Is that what you thought? That we wouldn't want you because you don't have a pristine past? If that was a requirement, none of us would be here—myself included! Of course we still want you! Now more than ever!"

The two women embraced, only to be interrupted by a nosy equine nudging his way between them. Both women planted a kiss on either side of Joey's head.

As the women walked to the parking lot, Sarah stopped suddenly.

"Oh, with all my emotional drama, I totally forgot to mention a fund-raising idea I thought of when I was doing barn chores."

"And what's your idea?"

"A poop-a-thon!" Sarah replied in all seriousness.

"A, uh, what now?"

"A poop-a-thon. You know, like a walk-a-thon, but with poop. Think about it. Horses make tons of poop, right? So why don't we have people sponsor volunteers to scoop? The more poop you scoop, the more money you raise! It's a win-win situation."

Kim couldn't help but laugh. The idea was unique, and it would surely get people talking. She grinned at her volunteer, who was staring expectantly at her.

"I'm all in. Let's do it."

CHAPTER 21

SARAH'S FUND-RAISING IDEA was definitely a hit. The first fund-raiser was such a success that now, a year later, the second annual Hope Reins Poop-a-Thon was in full swing, or rather full scoop. Kim stood in the middle of the property taking it all in—the squeals of laughter from delighted children, the sight of wheelbarrows being filled to the brim, and more volunteers than they had ever had. The number of people who were willing to give up their Saturday morning to shovel horse poop was remarkable. The local news had given them additional exposure with a story about the unusual fund-raiser.

Several people had already approached Kim, saying they wanted to start volunteering on a regular basis. She had wanted to hug each one and tell them how much they were needed. With Hope Reins coming up on its third year of operation, word was getting out, and they were receiving more session referrals than they had volunteers to staff. A waiting list had been created, and some families were having to wait several months before securing a session time.

While there was less worry about having funds for the day-to-day care of the horses, things were still tight. Kim hated the idea of turning families away who needed help, but without money to hire part-time session leaders, the responsibility fell on volunteers. Volunteers, especially those with horse experience, were hard to come by.

Kim couldn't say no to some of the recent referrals she had received. Calls such as the one from the widow of a soldier who took his own life after returning home from Iraq, whose two young children were now lost without their dad. Or the plea from a distraught mother whose six-year-old daughter had been sexually assaulted at her former school and was experiencing debilitating anxiety. Kim couldn't turn them away.

"Thank you, God, for providing," she whispered, after four different people told her they wanted to serve as session leaders.

The exuberant mayhem pulled Kim out of her thoughts. Sarah was showing a young boy how to effectively pick up a pile of manure with a pitchfork. *She's such a different person from a year and a half ago*, Kim marveled.

So much had changed since then. Joey had become the most requested horse at sessions, delighting children with his impressive list of vocal commands and his ability to be ridden bareback. Lauren had been placed on a new medication that seemed to be helping her pain a great deal. She was even serving as head trainer now. Aly was still reserved, but was talking more and more each time she came. She had brought a friend with her today—the two girls had bonded over a shared love of horses. And after her last session with Aly, Sarah had even told Kim that the little girl asked if someday she could ride Joey sitting backward! Apparently she had seen a YouTube video where a girl was sitting backward on a horse while being led around an arena. It seemed that little Aly had become quite fearless.

Yes, Sarah is flourishing. In fact, Kim was hoping that someday in the near future she could officially add the horse care and wellness position to the permanent staff and pay Sarah a salary. At the moment Sarah seemed quite content with things as they were, which possibly had something to do with a certain vet who was spending more and more of his free time at the ranch. Dr. Gallagher was all too eager to make ranch calls these days, and always seemed to need to consult with Sarah. Kim was truly delighted that the two were becoming good friends.

Kim's daughter ran over to her.

"Mama, come on. Come scoop some poop with us!"

How could she refuse that kind of fun?

———

Months later, on Christmas Eve morning, Kim found herself up earlier than planned. She had so much to do at home—food to prep, presents to wrap, and a house to clean—but she wanted to start her morning at Hope Reins. The sun had just crested the tree line, launching its glowing rays across the fields. The weather was chilly, but she knew she would warm up as she walked around.

A verse she had read the night before replayed in her mind. "But Mary treasured up all these things, pondering them in her heart." That's exactly what she was experiencing this morning, standing here at the ranch God had miraculously provided, among horses he had led them to, with the sweet memory of excited children's voices that would once again fill the fields in a few months. She had seen God do amazing things—life-changing, eternity-altering things—treasures she would always keep and ponder in her heart.

"God, you are so good," she prayed aloud. "I'm sorry that I doubt you so much. Thank you for providing this place, these horses, the kids and adults. Lord, you overwhelm me with your goodness and grace."

The cool air was invigorating. "This season is all about you. Let this place be all about you too—always. Let Hope Reins be a place where people can find you. Use this ministry to shine your light in a dark world. Use us, broken and sinful people, to point others to you."

As she continued her circuit, she prayed over each horse, over each child whose name she could remember, over every staff member and volunteer. She prayed for her family, for her friends, and for those who were hurting this season. Finally, her wandering ended at paddock two. She entered the gate and walked straight to the horse who held her heart.

"Hey, sweet boy," she greeted Joey, rubbing his neck just under his mane. His winter coat was thickening nicely.

"You are so beautiful," she said, leaning into the horse.

Joey rubbed his cheek against hers, just as he did when they first met on Tom's farm.

"What would we have done without you?" she wondered aloud. Of course, God would have still provided and moved in some other way, but she was grateful that he had chosen to work through the horse standing beside her.

"You are an answered prayer, you know that?" she said, placing a kiss on a large black spot. "It was a prayer I didn't even know I needed to pray, but God did. And he answered it with you, Joey—beautifully broken, yet completely whole. Merry Christmas."

CHAPTER 22

As CHRISTMAS GAVE WAY to New Year's and winter gave way to spring, Hope Reins was once again buzzing with activity. Thanks to the addition of several more volunteers, they had been able to increase the number of weekly sessions and help more families. Joey and Spirit had fallen into a comfortable companionship. All the horses were healthy at the moment.

The day after Easter, Aly had dazzled everyone by riding bareback and backward! She and Sarah had been working on it for several weeks. When they felt ready, Sarah asked Kim and Lauren to be there for Aly's session. She promised a surprise.

Kim's mouth had hung open for the entire demonstration—Aly trotting around the arena on Joey's back with Sarah holding on to the lead rope as a security measure.

When Aly was finished with her ride, Kim asked her why she had wanted to ride backward.

"Joey can't see where he's going, so I didn't want to see where I was going," she answered.

The tiny rider had a lot of wisdom at such a young age.

Now, as Kim walked to the office for a meeting with Barb, the recently designated vice president of Hope Reins, she noticed Lauren and Sarah standing with Joey. Their body language told her that something was wrong. She walked quickly toward the paddock.

"What's going on?" she called out as she entered the gate.

Sarah's brow furrowed. "I'm not sure. He's just not himself. I came out to check the water level in the trough and found him pawing hard at the ground. He didn't even seem to know I was here."

"I was with Deetz when Sarah texted me," Lauren said.

He does seem agitated, Kim thought. *Could it be colic?* Joey had been the healthiest horse in the herd. But now he was sweating profusely. Kim pulled out her phone to call Dr. Gallagher.

"I don't think Ryan has to be at work until noon today, so he should be able to come to the ranch," Sarah said, looking slightly embarrassed that she knew the veterinarian's schedule.

Kim, however, was quite grateful for the relationship that the two tried unsuccessfully to hide.

"Joey," Kim said softly, rubbing his cheek.

The horse's ears flicked at his name, then he stretched his head back toward his side. He straightened his neck for a minute and then forcefully thrust his head back to his side again. It was quite obvious that he was in pain.

The three women stayed with him until Dr. Gallagher arrived twenty minutes later. After they filled him in on what they had observed, the vet performed a quick examination—taking Joey's temperature and pulse, timing his respirations, and listening to his abdomen. He even walked Joey around the paddock to observe him in motion.

Dr. Gallagher told the concerned trio he suspected Joey might be having a mild colic episode—abdominal discomfort most likely due to gas.

Knowing how well Essie had responded to treatments, Kim was relieved. She knew that colic was common in horses, occurring for many different reasons. The majority of the time, medication took care of the problem. But colic could also be fatal, so every case was considered a potential emergency and had to be acted upon as quickly as possible.

"Let's watch him for now and see how he does the rest of the day," Dr. Gallagher advised. "I'll give him a dose of Banamine, which should help. And then I want you to walk him, at a slow to moderate pace, for about thirty minutes. Make sure he drinks plenty of water, and we'll make some changes to his diet. I'm hopeful this is a onetime episode that will resolve itself soon."

"And if not?" Kim asked, frightened of the answer.

Dr. Gallagher patted Joey's back.

"Then we will do everything we can to get this boy up and running again." He looked at Kim. "I really think this is a onetime happening. Try not to jump to worst-case scenarios right now."

The vet knew her too well.

"Keep me posted," he said, as Sarah accompanied him to his car. "I'll stop by on my way home this evening to check on him."

Kim and Lauren walked Joey around the paddock several times, grateful for something to do.

"Are you worried?" Lauren asked.

"I could lie and say no," Kim admitted, with a half-hearted laugh. "But truthfully, the idea of anything happening to Joey makes me panic."

She assessed the horse as he walked, relieved to find him looking and acting more like himself.

"I mean, he's Joey," Kim said, knowing that Lauren understood. "He's become such a fixture that it's hard to imagine Hope Reins without him."

One more lap and their thirty minutes would be up. Joey had passed gas percussively, and now he strained his head in search of Spirit, who was standing near the oak tree in the middle of the field. Joey seemed to be doing just fine. But Kim couldn't shake a feeling of apprehension.

Was this really a onetime thing? Or was something more serious happening to her dear friend?

Worry and trust. Would she ever cease battling for trust?

God, please let Joey be okay, she silently prayed as Lauren took Joey's halter off and he made his way to Spirit. *Please let this be as minor as Ryan thinks.* Then she forced herself to say the next words aloud: "But if not, Lord, please give us all the strength to face whatever lies ahead."

CHAPTER 23

THE SWEATING HORSE took a shaky step and then another. He craned his neck as far back as it would go and bumped his head against his side, nipping at the twisting pain in his abdomen. He tried to fight it. Tried to kick it away. But the pain continued to build. He bent his head low, twisted his neck, and then dropped to the earth in desperation, frantically rolling to escape from the pain.

His body violently thrashed around his familiar paddock. His head banged into the wooden hay box, and his hooves kicked a fence post. He heard a faint nicker nearby as well as other night sounds all around him, but the pain was too excruciating. He rolled again. And again. And again—frantically.

Dawn brought no relief, only the aftermath of his fight against the pain—dirt covered his coat, blood oozed from cuts on his head, leaves and hay were matted in his mane. Still he rolled, trying in vain to free himself from the torment.

"Dear Lord in heaven," the horse heard the human named Hank say. And then—for just a moment—all was quiet.

———•—•———

Lauren could not wrap her head around what was going on. Six months earlier, after Dr. Gallagher examined Joey and said that Joey had a minor, onetime incident of colic, Joey had bounced back almost immediately. She fought hard against the tidal wave of panic that threatened to wash her determination away. She couldn't lose it. Not now.

She slammed the door of her truck, wishing she could open it and slam it again and again until it came off its hinges. She headed down the path she had walked countless times over the past four years, since that first day when Speckles and Joey were unloaded. Her throat tightened. *No, no, no, Lauren*, she chastised herself. *You will not do this right now.* She forced herself to hurry, although she was terrified of what she would find. *Lord, I can't. I can't! Please help me*, she silently pleaded.

There he was. Standing just outside his paddock with Kim on one side and Barb on the other. Jo Anne and Hank stood in front of him. "Oh, Joey." The whispered cry escaped her lips. "What happened?"

His head was marred—deep cuts covered his head, neck, and back. Tremors of fear rippled through his muscles. In spite of the cool October morning, he was covered in sweat. Kim had said it was bad. And, dear God, it *was*.

Lauren had been at church when Kim called. The ranch founder never called on Sundays. Lauren instantly knew something was wrong. But what? She excused herself from the service to answer the phone.

"Lauren, we need you," Kim had said, unable to hide her distress. "Well, really Joey needs you. He won't get in the trailer, but he has to and we don't know how to make him. He's hurting and . . ."

Her words had tumbled out so fast that Lauren couldn't make sense of most of them, other than the words *Joey needs you.* That's all she needed to know.

"Lauren." Kim was still talking. "Hank found Joey rolling on the ground this morning. He was in terrible pain. Dr. Gallagher was just here and says it looks really serious. He said to meet him at the clinic with Joey as quickly as possible. It's been a nightmare, though. Joey's crying and keeps trying to roll. Whatever sedative Dr. Gallagher gave Joey to calm him down is not working. I honestly think it would help him to have you here."

Lauren had walked back into the sanctuary and motioned to her daughters that they needed to leave. She drove the girls home, quickly changed her clothes, and was at the ranch in less than thirty minutes.

Joey needed her, and she would be there.

A look of relief crossed Kim's face when she saw Lauren approach. She whispered something to Joey and waved Lauren over.

"Hey, Joe-Joe, love," Lauren said, stepping up to his face.

Joey's head jerked up. He whinnied, a mournful, terrified sound.

"Shhh, baby, I know it hurts. That's why we need to get you to the doctor."

"Is the trailer ready?" Lauren asked Barb.

"Yes, Hank hooked it up to the Tahoe. But we can't get Joey to move another step. It took us an hour just to move him out of his paddock. He keeps trying to go down."

Tears pooled in Barb's eyes. Everyone's face reflected the emotional strain of the situation.

"Okay, my friend," Lauren said to Joey, taking his large head gently in her hands. "We are going to go nice and slow to the trailer. I know you're scared, so you just follow me."

She held his muzzle—one hand on each side of his face—and took a step back, keeping her eyes on him. She inhaled loudly, then forcibly exhaled as she stepped, praying the sound resembled that of a relaxed horse. Praying that the familiar sound would help calm Joey. He stepped forward as she stepped back. She exaggerated the sound even more, Joey's head still resting in her hands. They continued their slow movement across the ranch.

"Lauren, the bond you two have is extraordinary. Joey feels so safe with you," Kim said, encouraging her lead trainer.

Lauren's gaze never left Joey as she replied, "The feeling is mutual."

Joey occasionally stopped to thrash his head and let out a loud cry. Lauren would begin talking quietly to him, sometimes even softly singing "Amazing Grace" or "Jesus Loves Me"—anything to try to get his head turned back to her. Then she would begin moving again.

It took thirty minutes to cross from the paddock to the trailer and another thirty minutes to get the agitated, terrified horse loaded onto the vehicle. Joey had not been in a confined space for more than four years. To Lauren's knowledge, Joey had never entered the run-in shelter in the paddock. Small spaces seemed to scare him.

Lauren secured Joey, then shimmied out of the tight space, closed the trailer door, and jumped into the Tahoe behind Kim and Barb. Barb slowly maneuvered the SUV and trailer down the gravel drive, and Lauren turned around to look at paddock two.

Fear filled her heart. *Joey might never be coming back.* Kim was on the phone with Sarah, who was at a training seminar about an hour away. Lauren listened as Kim explained what had happened to Joey. When she finished the call, Kim's eyes were glistening and she grabbed Lauren's hand. For the rest of the ride, the three women prayed without ceasing.

Sarah sped into the parking lot at the vet school. It had taken her two hours to get here. *Of all the weekends to have been away.* She saw the Tahoe with the trailer parked in the back spaces. She hurried from the car, checked in with the receptionist, and raced back to the stall where she knew Joey would be. *How did they ever get him in there?* She turned a corner and came to a halt.

Joey? He looked so sick. His head hung over the stall door. He was covered in sweat and hooked up to a long IV line. Lauren's face was pressed against Joey's. Kim and Barb stood behind Lauren, holding on to each other. Sarah was afraid to announce herself. Her limbs grew heavy, her fingers tingled, and her head buzzed. She hadn't experienced anxiety in such a long time. But how could she feel anything but anxious right now?

Finally, Sarah whispered, "How is he?"

Two tearstained faces met hers. Lauren did not turn around, did not take her eyes off Joey. Kim shook her head slightly and motioned for Sarah to come closer, wrapping an arm around her.

"It's not good," Kim said. "There is nothing they can do for him."

Wait. What? What! Sarah immediately tensed up and pulled away.

"Nothing they can do?" she all but shouted, feeling her

control slipping away. "What do you mean? What's going on? Where's Ryan?"

None of this made any sense. Joey was fine. He had been fine. She had just been with him two days ago. Surely someone had made a huge mistake.

This wasn't like Speckles. He had been sick; they had known that. But this was Joey. Joey was fine.

"Severe colic." Kim winced at the words.

"Yes, horses get colic," Sarah interrupted, feeling completely frustrated. "Joey had that minor episode several months ago. We just needed to change his supplements. We can do that again, right?" She shook her head, willing Kim to see reason. Why was she so freaked out? This wasn't a big deal. What was everyone's problem?

Kim placed her hand on Sarah's arm.

"Ryan and the other four vets believe that Joey likely has a tumor wrapped around his stomach, cutting off his digestive tract. It's a complete blockage that is hard to reach. And with Joey's limitations, surgery really isn't an option."

Kim looked at Joey. "He's terrified being confined here. Can you imagine making him stay here for weeks, recovering from a surgery that most likely won't even work? They have a few more tests to run, but Ryan said to be prepared for some hard decisions."

No! Sarah wanted to scream. *This cannot be happening. Not again. Please . . . not to Joey.* She wanted to run. *I have to get away.*

Joey's head jerked out of Lauren's hands. A cry escaped his lips. Lauren and Barb each began to stroke his face, immovable buttresses, supporting and comforting the hurting horse, standing with the one who had taught them so much.

Sarah's heart raced as she made her way to Joey, not stopping until she stood nose to nose with him. He recognized her scent, and she took in his.

"I gotcha, Joey. I'm here for you," she whispered. They were the same promises she'd made the first time she met him, injured and bloodied. "I promise. I will not leave you."

It was time. Lauren knew it in her gut. But how could she possibly let Joey go? He had seen her through the crushing grief of losing Speckles just years before and helped her begin to live again. What would she do without him?

Dr. Gallagher opened the door to the stall. Joey stood in the small room, looking so lost, so tired.

When Kim, Barb, Sarah, and Lauren entered the stall, Joey turned his head, clearly aware of their presence, and yet slipping away. Lauren knew that Joey would be taking a piece of her heart when he left this world. Joey had taught her what real courage looked like: moving forward even when you can't see the road in front of you by trusting the one who is leading you.

The massive amounts of painkillers had quieted him somewhat, but he was still sweating profusely and experiencing regular muscle spasms. He was in agony. The four women silently gathered around the beloved horse, each lost in her own thoughts. One by one, they laid their hands on the horse who had touched them all in profound ways.

Kim began praying aloud.

"Lord, we need you. We need your Spirit of peace, comfort, and hope. God, we can't say good-bye to this boy." Her voice broke. Barb hugged Kim close. "Father, we thank you for Joey. Thank you for preserving his life when he was abandoned, in order to bring him to us." As Kim prayed, Joey became agitated.

Lauren could tell that he wanted to drop to the ground and roll. She moved in front of him and touched her nose to his. Then she placed one hand on Joey's forehead and one low on his muzzle.

Inhale.

Exhale.

Inhale.

Exhale.

Kim continued to pray. "God, so many people are going to be heartbroken over the loss of this extraordinary horse. Please comfort all of us, especially the kids who love Joey so much."

Joey now stood perfectly still.

"God, we don't understand why you are allowing this, but we choose to trust you, to walk in blind faith beside you."

As Kim uttered a shaky amen, Sarah began to sing:

Amazing grace! How sweet the sound
That saved a wretch like me!
I once was lost, but now am found,
Was blind, but now I see.

The other three women joined in on the last line, each clinging to the hope that Joey would soon see once again.

Joey's head jerked up as his legs began to bend. His eyes were wide, his jaw tight.

"It's time," Sarah said quietly.

Dr. Gallagher nodded and began preparing the final dose of barbiturates.

Lauren looked at Joey. "You did so much good. Now it is time for you to rest—and to see."

"We love you, Joey," each one of them said.

"You will never be forgotten," Sarah whispered.

As Dr. Gallagher injected the barbiturates into the IV, Lauren rubbed Joey's chin one last time. "My sweet Joey." She choked out the words as she wept. "Good-bye, my love."

CHAPTER 24

THE LOSS OF JOEY RIPPLED far and wide across the Hope Reins community. Children and adults, staff and volunteers, those familiar with the ranch and others who had just heard the story of the remarkable blind horse were now connected in sorrow. All were longing to *do* something, looking to honor the horse in some way. Messages of sympathy, cards containing special memories of Joey, and pictures of a spotted horse drawn in crayon poured into the ranch. For a week, Kim, Sarah, and Lauren grieved together privately, often finding themselves standing and reflecting in paddock two, just to feel close to Joey. Finally, the staff knew it was time to plan a memorial service to pay tribute to the horse who had touched so many lives.

"Do you think anyone will come?" Sarah asked during their first planning meeting.

"Based on the messages I've received, yes, I do," Kim said.

"But even if only a few show up, it will be worth it. We need to do this—for us, for them, and for Joey."

Kim, Sarah, and Barb compiled a list of assignments and created a program. Kim kept wanting to ask Lauren's opinion, but the head trainer had not been at the ranch for several days. Joey's death had hit her especially hard; she needed more time. Kim intended to let her know everything they discussed and hoped Lauren would come to the service on Saturday.

As the meeting concluded, Kim gazed out the office window. Spirit had been moved back in with Gabe, so paddock two was empty. Would another horse ever call that field home?

The weather on that Saturday in October 2014 was picture perfect—not a cloud in the sky. The Hope Reins staff couldn't have asked for a better day to celebrate Joey's life. He had taught all who knew him what it meant to find beauty in brokenness, purpose in pain, light in darkness. The size of the crowd at his memorial service was a testament to how many people had been affected by the horse who had nearly been thrown away.

The Hope Reins staff had done a great job pulling the event together. Children ran carefree across the ranch, expressing the same kind of joy that the rescued horse had given them. Photos of the beautiful leopard Appaloosa had been arranged on tables in the common area, and Kim watched as people lingered in front of the images, pointing and smiling before wiping tears away. They knew firsthand the significant contribution Joey had made to the success of Hope Reins. Black-and-white balloons were tied to the legs of the tables, and paper was available for people to write personal messages.

Finally, it was time to begin. Kim welcomed everyone sitting in the common area, recognizing many familiar faces. Ethan, the first boy to ever work with Joey, sat in the front row. Jo Anne and Hank, the feeders who had found Joey that awful morning, stood on one side. Aly, next to her mother, was rubbing her hands on her jeans. She had just come from Joey's run-in shelter, where she had traced "Aly and Joey 4-ever" in the sand. There was Nathan, whom Joey had "introduced" to his seeing-eye horse, Speckles. Kim saw her Hope Reins team spread throughout the crowd, all smiling at her in support. And there, standing behind everyone else, was Lauren.

Thank you, God, for helping Lauren to be here.

Kim took a deep breath and began, "Friends, thank you all so much for coming out today to honor a special horse. As you know, Joey was more than a horse. He was a light and an example. And he was God's gift to us."

Heads throughout the crowd nodded in agreement.

"For those who were blessed to know Joey, and extra blessed to be loved *by* him, you know that Joey's life had a purpose. Every day, that horse stood in his field, or walked beside a child, or followed his trainer in blind faith. Faith that he would be cared for, faith that he would be led to safety, faith that he would never again be abandoned."

She paused for a moment to fight back tears, then continued. "Friends, God used a blind horse to teach us what it means to walk by faith. He used a broken horse to show us what it means to heal. And he used a dying horse to show us how we should live. Joey is gone, and we all miss him terribly. But Joey lives on in every one of us."

She took a step forward to be a little closer to those hurting with her.

"Each time we choose to walk in faith, holding tightly to God's hand, Joey's legacy lives on. Each time we choose trust over fear, Joey's memory is kept alive. And even in our grief, as we press on like Joey did after the death of his best friend, Speckles, we honor his life. As we go from here today, let's continue to shine God's light—his hope and his comfort—into this world. That can be our fitting tribute to Joey."

Just then, a horse neighed in the background, the solitary sound poetic and oddly comforting.

"And now, please welcome Aly, one of Joey's friends."

Aly, now eight years old, got up and stood in front of Kim, who put her hands firmly on the young equestrian's shoulders. Kim had promised Aly that she would stand with her. The paper clutched in Aly's hand was filled with words written in purple ink.

Aly looked at Kim and began to read. "I met Joey when I was five years old, and I loved him right away. When I was six years old, I finally got to ride him. I was very shy, but somehow I grew a big friendship with Joey."

Her soft voice trembled slightly, but it sounded angelic to Kim.

"Joey respected me," Aly continued, "and I respected him, too. Since Joey was blind, I had to speak up when I rode him. This was really hard for me, but I guess you could say Joey helped me find my voice."

Kim smiled. *And find it you did.* Over the years, Aly had brought countless friends to the ranch to meet Joey, and they all had become fans of the spotted horse.

"While riding Joey, I learned how to steer a horse, ride bareback, and give commands. And," she said, smiling broadly, "I learned how to make a horse hug me by holding a treat and moving it around my neck."

Aly wrapped one arm around herself as she spoke, surely longing to feel just one more hug from Joey.

"One day at Hope Reins, Joey gave me a big kiss on the cheek!" She looked up at Kim. "I'm glad Joey got to live the end of his life at Hope Reins because he deserved happiness. I miss Joey very much, and he will always have a special place in my heart."

Sarah, who had grabbed Ryan's hand the moment Aly stepped up to speak, now dried her tears on the sleeve of his shirt. Images of that first meeting with Aly flashed through her memory. Aly had been so silent, so withdrawn, so trapped. But now she was fearless. Now she was free. *Just like me, Aly.* God used a blind horse to help a silent girl, who helped a wounded woman. She snuggled against Ryan's arm. *Thank you, Joey,* she mouthed.

Aly gave Kim a hug and then returned to her seat beside her mother. There were lots of tears during Aly's speech, and some were in awe—those who knew the magnitude of what Aly had accomplished by addressing this crowd. It was a powerful testimony of God working in ordinary people, through an ordinary horse.

Kim once again got everyone's attention. "I'm sure you noticed the balloons at the tables. Today, we are designating them 'memory balloons.' I invite any of you who would like to write a note of thanks to Joey, draw a picture, or share a memory to use the paper provided, and we'll attach it to a balloon. Or feel free to use a permanent marker to write your message directly on the balloon. Take a few minutes to do that, and then bring your balloons to paddock two."

Fifteen minutes later, Kim stood in the middle of Joey's field and led the group in prayer.

"Lord, we thank you for Joey's life. Thank you for giving us time with him. We miss him greatly, and we ask that you help us through this difficult time. Help us to love and accept others as Joey did. Help us to trust you in blind faith and total surrender, just as Joey trusted us. You are a God of hope and of healing. We love you, Lord, and we praise you for the opportunity to love our sweet boy."

As she said amen, more than fifty balloons—signifying black-and-white polka dots—were released heavenward.

All for a horse named Joey.

EPILOGUE

THE HORSE WAS SKIN AND BONES, and yet she was gorgeous. A wide white patch ran the length of her muzzle, the brilliant white in stark contrast to her copper-colored coat and strawberry blonde mane. She whinnied and shook her head, obviously nervous and fearful.

"It's okay, sweet girl," Kim crooned. "You're safe. This is your new home." The mare's eyes were wide set—common for a Saddlebred, yet making her look more terrified. "You have a lot of people waiting to meet you. How about we get out of this trailer and go meet your new family?"

The horse stomped the trailer's floor. Kim unhooked her from the ties and attached a lead rope to her halter.

The animal had been rescued from a horrific situation. Of the forty horses seized from a Saddlebred horse hoarder, she was one of just eleven that had survived. The only information Kim had about the horse was that her early training had involved traumatic methods—the use of chains and firecrackers to force her into the high-stepping paces desired in the competition ring. The horse was scarred—physically and emotionally—from the cruel practices and unimaginable neglect, and yet she had survived. Surely she was a fighter.

Kim's throat tightened with emotion. Hope Reins now had a Saddlebred. *She* had a Saddlebred. How many years had she longed for a horse just like Country, her childhood friend? After all these years, Kim was going to get her wish. This Saddlebred would never be forced to do anything she didn't want to do. She would simply be loved here.

Kim backed her out of the trailer. The horse's steps were unsure, her ears pricked on high alert.

Oohs and aahs erupted from the crowd of staff and volunteers waiting for their first peek at the newest Hope Reins resident.

"Kim, she's beautiful!" Sarah exclaimed.

Kim and Barb had agreed to give her a permanent home, sight unseen. The only other horse they had done that for was Joey.

Joey.

A pang of sadness gripped Kim's heart for a moment. The loss was still palpable. Hardly a day went by without someone mentioning his name. But life went on, as it always did. They were all adjusting to a new normal. And then, three weeks ago, Kim had gotten the call about this horse.

Lauren let the horse sniff her hand. "Well, hi there," she said, before turning to Kim. "What are you going to call her?"

Kim had thought about that a lot. They often gave Hope Reins horses new names. It seemed fitting to get a new name with a new life. Of course, sometimes they kept the horse's original name, as in Joey's case. But Kim believed this mare deserved a significant, meaningful name to make up for the terrible abuse she had suffered. Kim had been talking it over with Mike and praying about it.

A week earlier, she read Psalm 3 for her morning devotions and saw a word repeated three times: *Selah*. Kim researched its meaning and found that most scholars agreed it meant "to pause, rest, and reflect." It took Kim back to that Christmas Eve morning one year before, when she sat at the ranch with Joey pondering—pausing and reflecting—on God's goodness.

"This is Selah," Kim announced to the Hope Reins team. "She needs a pause in her life. She needs to rest, and we need to reflect on all that God has done for and through this ministry."

The look of delight on everyone's face confirmed that she had chosen well.

Kim could already imagine the lives Selah was going to touch. This horse had survived the worst life had to offer, but she was still standing. Still breathing. Still living. Kim knew that children and adults would relate to her fearful distrust of people, and she hoped that as they helped to rebuild that trust for Selah, they might rebuild some of their own.

She prayed that God would somehow use this broken horse to bring healing to others. And she suspected that of all the people Selah's life would touch, her own would be affected most of all. In the brief time she had known this horse, she had seen so much of her own story reflected in Selah's. Yes, this horse was special.

"Where are we taking Selah?" Sarah asked, admiring the new equine counselor.

It seemed Kim's soul had been waiting to answer that question for months. "Paddock two."

"To know Joey was to love Joey."

This was a phrase I heard often during my interviews with people who had the honor of spending time with Joey. Some shared treasured memories, others recalled amusing incidents, many offered thoughtful reflections, and all agreed that you couldn't help but love this beautiful horse. I hope that you will get to know Joey just a little better through these images.

Heidi Grable, one of Joey's beloved trainers,
painted this remarkable likeness of him.

With no money for advertising when Hope Reins first opened, this appealing sign drew families in.

With such a soulful gaze, it was hard to believe that Joey was actually blind.

Speckles eventually learned that sharing makes everyone happy.

It didn't take long for Joey and Speckles to become inseparable.

Before beginning
sessions, the
volunteers always
gathered for prayer.

The tack shed (left)
and feed shed (right)
were conveniently
located near the
hitching posts.

Grooming the horse
is an important part
of each session.
Here, Hilary, a session
leader, steadied Joey
for brushing.

Joey was great at boosting a child's self-confidence because of his easygoing manner.

Joey never lacked for attention!

Everyone agreed that Joey and Speckles were made for each other.

Several training methods proved effective with Joey, and he was a star pupil.

Aly bonded with Joey the first time she met him.

Joey loved getting and giving hugs.

The common area—a spacious gathering place for events, with the small office nestled under the trees in the background on the right.

Joey was a willing canvas for summer camp kids to finger paint in natural hues. He loved the hands-on artists!

Spirit (foreground) and Joey at home in paddock two.

In many ways, Selah, a rescued Saddlebred, has been God's personalized gift to Kim.

Author's Note

I AM NOT A HORSE PERSON, nor did I ever dream of writing a book about a horse.

But then I met Joey.

The extent of my horse experience before then had consisted of a trail ride at the age of nine. But as a former grief counselor to children and families, I was intrigued by the work Kim Tschirret was doing at Hope Reins, and I wanted to learn more about the ministry. I gladly accepted an invitation to attend a fund-raising dinner in 2012.

That night, as our group approached paddock two, I was busy thinking about how I might be able to serve at the horse ranch. Lost in my thoughts, I was startled by a horse's head stretching over the fence in search of a carrot Kim was holding. I remember staring at Joey's midnight-black eyes as Kim shared his story. It seemed as if the horse could see into my soul.

Normally, I am timid around horses, yet I found myself reaching my hand out toward Joey as Kim spoke. He touched my hand the moment she said the word *blind*.

My hand froze as I stared into his eyes. I could hear Kim in the background, elaborating on Joey's impact at Hope Reins, but I was completely mesmerized by the horse standing in front of me.

A dinner bell rang, signaling the end of our ranch tour. Everyone started heading to the large white tent where a delicious dinner would be served. Yet I could not move. The sun was setting in brilliant hues that evening, all the beautiful colors reflected in Joey's eyes.

At that moment, God stirred my heart to write Joey's story. It made no sense to me. I had zero horse experience. How was I supposed to write a book about a horse? I was just there to learn more about the ministry. I left that night full of excitement and uncertainty—longing to write his story, yet feeling completely unqualified to do so.

Over the next few weeks, I found myself thinking of Joey. Eventually, I began driving by the ranch just to catch a glimpse of him. I arranged to interview the people who had known and worked with Joey, asking them countless questions. I read dozens of books about horses and did other research. And then, months after that first meeting, I began to type.

Writing Joey's story was not easy. At times I couldn't see where I was headed or how I was going to get there. But maybe, just maybe, that was part of God's plan all along. Crafting Joey's story inspired me to write more, something I had always loved to do but had put aside for many years. Yes, just as Joey helped Aly to become less timid and find her voice, he also did that for me.

Acknowledgments

I have always loved reading acknowledgment pages because they provide a window into an author's life and process. Yet before writing a book, I could never understand how an author could have so many people to thank.

Well, now I know! In fact, I truly believe I could write an entire book of thank-yous to everyone who contributed to this project.

Kim Tschirret, I admire your obedience to God's call to start Hope Reins in order to help hurting children find hope. You are the real deal, and I am grateful and honored to call you my friend.

Thanks to all the amazing people at Hope Reins, especially Barb Foulkrod, Jennifer Shepard, Elizabeth Love, and Jo Anne Mailand, for being willing to answer my countless questions. Every time I e-mailed or texted a question, you were so quick to respond! Thank you for being patient with me and forgiving me for my lack of horse experience. And Jen and Elizabeth, thank you for letting me shadow both of you. I learned so much about horses *and life* from you two!

Heidi, how many questions did I send you? I lost count. But

you answered each and every one. Thank you for inviting me into your home and into your memories.

To Lacy, Joan, Penny, Lisa, and Todd: It was a privilege to hear the role each of you played in Joey's life before he found his way to Hope Reins. You helped build a foundation of trust that enabled him to triumph over his circumstances. I'm glad I could tell you about his remaining productive years. On behalf of all who were forever changed by Joey, thank you for loving him so well.

To Jessica Kirkland, my incredibly talented agent: I was a genre orphan when I called you with my story idea. I had no idea what I had written. You listened intently, and you gave *Joey* (and me) a home. Your vision for this project was far bigger than my own, and I am forever grateful.

To the Tyndale Momentum team: Sarah Atkinson, Carol Traver, Bonne Steffen, Jillian Schlossberg, Kara Leonino, Sharon Leavitt, and everyone else involved. I thought having my book published would be the highlight of this experience, but honestly, it has been meeting and getting to learn from all of you. (Don't get me wrong, the whole publishing thing is pretty cool too!) Sarah, you made me feel welcome from that first phone call. Thank you for loving Joey's story and for taking a chance on a blind horse and an unknown author. The moment I discovered you were a dog person, I knew *Joey* was in good hands! Carol, if Joey had a guardian angel, she would have your face, your giftedness with story structure, and an adorable cat! *Thank you* hardly seems adequate to express the depth of gratitude I have for you and what you did for this book. Bonne, it was a joy to work with you. If Carol was Joey's guardian angel, you were mine! You tightened and tweaked the manuscript to make it stronger (especially in those chapters where we could hardly see through the tears!).

To Margot Starbuck: What a joy to get to know you and work with you. You guided me through the entire writing process, and it was a delightful experience. I am indebted to you for your tireless work in the beginning (hello, point of view and story structure) and for your constant encouragement. I am blessed to know you.

Mike Hall, thank you for giving me a chance to write curriculum all those years ago. At the time, it made no sense, but then again, you have always marched to your own drum! God used you to rekindle a passion within me for the written word that blossomed in this book.

Jennifer Sharpe and Megan Lawrence: You were my first editors, and I learned so much from both of you. Thank you for your friendship, support, and prayers.

None of this would have been possible without the unwavering support of my family and friends who prayed for me and sent me words of encouragement and pictures to make me laugh. Aimee, Julie, Melissa, Kat, Crystal, Lindy, Kathryn, Tana, Lori, and Nicole: Every time I would hit the proverbial wall, God would urge one of you in my direction with just what I needed to go on. Each one of you is a precious friend to me.

To all my friends at LAMBS: Thank you for caring about this project and praying diligently for it.

To Aunt Judy: Every time I called with a *Joey* update, your excitement rivaled, if not exceeded, my own. You are my own personal cheerleader, and I am so thankful for you.

To Mom and Daddy: I hit the jackpot when it came to my parents! You have always made me believe that I can do anything God calls me to do. Thank you for continually pointing me to the hope I have in Jesus. And Daddy, thank you for writing notes to your shy little girl, who found it difficult to verbalize what was in my heart. Your notes—and encouragement to write back to you—provided me with a way to share my thoughts and feelings. In many ways you unlocked my voice, and I am forever grateful.

To my precious tribe: Darrell, Andrew, and Ella, none of this would have happened without you three. Your enthusiasm and understanding kept me going (even though I did not always keep the laundry or cooking going!). You are my safe place—you are my home. I love you more than I can express. Darrell, thank you for your unwavering devotion. Thank you for telling me that I could do this. Andrew and Ella, I love making up stories for you. You will always be my favorite audience. I love all of you for eternity times infinity and beyond!

And last, but certainly not least, Father God, none of this would have happened if not for you. I will never understand why you chose me to do this, but Lord, I am so grateful you did. I went to the ranch that day looking for a place to connect, and I found a calling instead. Jesus, you are my light, my love, and my life. You are my hope. This is all about you. Joey was your horse, this has always been your story, and I am forever your girl.

Much love,

Jen

Group Discussion Questions

1. When Hope Reins founder Kim Tschirret met Joey, the abandoned Appaloosa, she instantly knew he belonged at her therapy ranch despite the extra care he required. Have you ever made a decision that made no sense to anyone but yourself? Did it turn out to be a good decision or not?

2. The deep connection between animals and people has spawned countless therapeutic organizations that have truly made a difference in the participants' quality of life. Have you ever experienced that kind of connection with your own personal pet? Why do you think there is such a bond?

3. Kim was inspired to start Hope Reins after reading another woman's story of successfully pursuing the same dream. Do you have an unfulfilled dream that you can't dismiss? What prevents you from seeing it realized?

4. The words of 2 Corinthians 1:3-4 became a catalyst for Kim to start Hope Reins: "God is our merciful Father and the source of all comfort. He comforts us in all our

troubles so that we can comfort others." Have you ever been able to extend special comfort to someone because you had been through a situation similar to theirs?

5. God miraculously provided the land for Hope Reins through the generosity of a local church. Can you think of any generous, but unexpected, gifts (material or otherwise) you have received?

6. As the day-to-day demands of running the ranch began to pile up, Kim held on to the mantra "God will provide." Have you ever found yourself repeating that same mantra to yourself? In what ways did God provide for you?

7. Although Kim believed that God would meet all of the ranch's needs, she struggled with worry, trying her best to change it to trust. Can you identify with that struggle in your life? What has helped you move from worry to trust?

8. When Joey got tangled up in the electric wire fencing and was injured, Kim shouldered all the blame. But her staff members rallied with encouraging support so Kim wouldn't be overcome by the what-ifs. Have you ever been emotionally paralyzed by regret and what-ifs? How did you get going again?

9. Lauren took a risk when she faced off with Speckles, reprimanding him for his treatment of Joey. Almost immediately she had second thoughts about the wisdom of her decision, but she didn't back down. To her amazement, Speckles did, and that moment started the horse and trainer in a positive direction. Have you ever

taken a risk that seemed foolish, but turned out better than you imagined possible?

10. Sarah witnessed Lauren working with Speckles and said, "Maybe Speckles needs us to understand how his past affects his present." As the story unfolds, you realize that the horses aren't the only ones who have been injured in some way in the past—people have too. What about you? Is something in your past affecting your present? What steps of healing do you need to take? Is there someone you may have judged too quickly, without the benefit of knowing his or her complete story?

11. When Ethan asked Sarah if she believed in God, a lot of things went through her mind before she answered. Would you have answered Ethan's question differently?

12. As Speckles and Joey became inseparable, the trainers realized that the horses' bond defined their purpose. Speckles may not have been able to be ridden like the other therapy horses on the ranch, but he still had a purpose by serving as Joey's eyes. Have you ever wondered what your purpose on earth is? Has your purpose changed at different times of your life?

13. Would you agree with Kim that "walking in blind faith is not for wimps"?

14. Both Lauren and Joey grieved when Speckles died, forming their own support group. Joey's physical presence became a way for Lauren to experience God's invisible presence. Both helped her begin to heal. Has God ever

displayed his presence in surprising ways that brought you closer to him?

15. Following a period of intense grief and adjustment, Joey once again began to thrive—learning vocal commands, carrying a rider without a lead line, and helping Aly find her voice. Have you suffered a significant loss that makes it difficult to see past the pain? Do you find encouragement from Joey's grief process and renewed purpose following Speckles' death? What new joy and purpose might await you in this new season?

16. After witnessing Aly's breakthrough with Joey, Sarah faced her own fears and opened up to Kim. Have you ever been scared to share the real you with someone for fear of rejection? Do you agree with Kim's statement that "all of us are works in progress"? How might this realization help us relate more truthfully to one another?

ARE YOU ON GOODREADS?

Be sure to mark *Joey* "Currently Reading" or "Read."

If you enjoyed this book . . . consider adding it to the following lists:

- Animal Memoirs
- Best Books About Animals
- Best Animal Books
- Horse Books/Novels
- Best Christian Fiction and Nonfiction
- Best Horse Books
- Horse Lover's Literature

If you have questions for the author, be sure to visit Jennifer Bleakley's author page and connect with her online to enhance your book club or personal reading experience!

Also available from Tyndale House Publishers

The heartwarming true tale of an irrepressible donkey who needed a home—and forever changed a family.

An uplifting story of a man and his lovable Labs, who helped him discover enduring truths about love, grace, and gratitude.

One man's resolve to live in the moment and celebrate the ways God reveals himself every day.

HOPE LIVES HERE.

Enter the gates of Hope Reins and discover a 33-acre ranch where God masterfully intersects the hearts of a dedicated team of people and an amazing herd of rescued horses with the sole mission of supporting hurting kids. *Hope lives here*. And so did our beloved Joey.

His story is one of darkness and light. Darkness because Joey suffered starvation and blindness. But his amazing perseverance and triumph over adversity lit a path of hope and healing for hundreds of hurting kids and families at the ranch.

Hope Reins is a nonprofit ministry in Raleigh, North Carolina, dedicated to comforting emotionally wounded kids aged 5–18. Many of our "equine counselors" faced abuse or neglect themselves, and this shared story of pain helps open and heal the hearts of kids. All of our services are free of charge. *Join us!*

HOPE REINS
True Hope. Real Healing.

www.hopereinsnc.org

CP1356